P9-DTV-312

RENEWALS 458-4574

WORKING WITH
Sex Offenders

WORKING WITH
Sex Offenders
GUIDELINES FOR THERAPIST SELECTION

MICHAEL A. O'CONNELL • ERIC LEBERG
CRAIG R. DONALDSON

Foreword by Anna C. Salter

SAGE PUBLICATIONS
The International Professional Publishers
Newbury Park   London   New Delhi

Copyright © 1990 by Sage Publications, Inc.

All rights reserved. No part of this book may be reproduced or utilized in any form or by any means, electronic or mechanical, including photocopying, recording, or by any information storage and retrieval system, without permission in writing from the publisher.

For information address:

SAGE Publications, Inc.
2111 West Hillcrest Drive
Newbury Park, California 91320

SAGE Publications Ltd.
28 Banner Street
London EC1Y 8QE
England

SAGE Publications India Pvt. Ltd.
M-32 Market
Greater Kailash I
New Delhi 110 048 India

Printed in the United States of America

Library of Congress Cataloging-in-Publication Data

O'Connell, Michael A.
    Working with sex offenders : guidelines for therapist selection /
by Michael A. O'Connell, Eric Leberg, Craig R. Donaldson.
        p. cm.
    Includes biographical references.
    ISBN 0-8039-3754-7. -- ISBN 0-8039-3763-6 (pbk.)
    1. Sex offenders--Rehabilitation.   2. Psychotherapists--Selection
and appointment.   3. Community mental health services.   I. Leberg,
Eric.   II. Donaldson, Craig R.   III. Title.
RC560.S47026   1990
616.85'83--dc20   89-24243
                                                           CIP

FIRST PRINTING, 1990

LIBRARY
The University of Texas
at San Antonio

Contents

Foreword
by Anna C. Salter

Sexual abuse has truly been, in Florence Rush's words, "the best kept secret." Although research since the 1920s has consistently documented a high prevalence of sexual abuse, the information has been largely ignored by professionals and seldom made available to the public (Salter, 1988). A convenient theory was used to explain the numbers of adult women complaining of sexual abuse as children. They were victims, not of sex offenders, but of Oedipal fantasies (Masson, 1984). Those adults and children who were acknowledged to have been abused frequently found themselves blamed for the attacks. Abraham wrote in 1927 that

> Female hysterics in particular are constantly meeting with adventures. They are molested in the public street, outrageous sexual assaults are made on them, etc. It is part of their nature that they must expose themselves to external traumatic influences. There is in them a need to appear to be constantly subjected to external violence. In this we recognize a general psychological characteristic of women in an exaggerated form. (p. 57)

Throughout this century young child victims have been frequently described as "seductive" or "provocative" (e.g., Mohr, Turner, & Jerry, 1964; Revitch & Weiss, 1962; Virkkunen, 1975). The clinical basis for these observations were sometimes interviews with the offender alone. Revitch and Weiss (1962) noted that, "We rarely had the opportunity of examining the victims of pedophiles; however, we have the clinical impression that quite often the child victim is aggressive and seductive and often induces the adult offender to commit the offense" (p. 74). In a 1981 article Virkkunen implied the offender's word should be taken over the official records in a study in which the two differed as to the degree of "victim participation."

Under such circumstances there could be little interest in treating sex offenders. Some authors, in fact, suggested that it was the "participating victims" who were in need of treatment. "Unlike most other sex crimes the male offender in the case of statutory rape has no special pathology; the girl is usually more in need of psychiatric care or other attention" (Slovenko, 1971).

Clearly professional denial and community denial were the order of the century. By this point Florence Rush (1980), Judith Herman (1981), Jeffrey Masson (1984) and others have eloquently documented the breadth and depth of this denial. In the last five years, due to efforts such as theirs and to the extraordinary phenomena of adult survivors beginning to say the unthinkable out loud and in public, this denial has begun to weaken. With the recognition of the widespread nature of child sexual abuse and adult sexual assault, however, a backlash has developed whose proponents insist that the phenomenon has been exaggerated. Silence has been replaced by vocal opposition (Hechler, 1987).

But the unthinkable has been said, and not everyone will vote to suppress it. Reliable research finds the prevalence of child sexual abuse of females to be from 28 to 38% of the population, depending on whether you study girls under 14 or under 18 (Russell, 1984). Almost half (44%) of the adult women in Russell's methodologically sound study had been the victims of either rape or attempted rape.

With the admission of the prevalence of sexual abuse and the beginning of widespread sex offender treatment programs, the chronicity and repetitiveness of sexual aggression without treatment has begun to be recognized. Abel et al. (1987) found that the average female-oriented pedophile had 20 victims and the average male-oriented pedophile 150. In their voluntary and confidential study, 232 child molesters admitted to having over 17,000 victims under the age of 14. When all types of paraphiliac acts were included 561 sex offenders admitted to over 291,000 deviant acts with a total of over 195,000 victims.

With the lessening of community denial and a beginning recognition of the compulsiveness of sexual aggression has come a new interest in treating sex offenders. But what kind of treatment by practitioners with what types of credentials? The judge, probation and parole officer, the child protection worker, the administrator will look in vain through the literature for a guide. What has been missing previously in the field is a guide to selecting therapists with the appropriate credentials and training to treat sex offenders, an explanation of the components that should go into an appropriate evaluation, a description of the external controls that must be placed on sex offenders for community based treatment to work, and an over-view of the components which comprise treatment. There is a growing consensus within the field as to the necessity for specialized sex offender evaluation and treatment but no published standards for those selected programs and personnel.

There is a need for such standards. The professional attempting to select a program or personnel for a program will often find contradictory presentations by groups each proporting to evaluate and treat sex offenders. Recently I received a call from a court administrator. Someone had made a presentation to a group of judges and promised to "fix" sex offenders for a set amount per person with the use of family therapy. The offender did not have to leave the home, and the family, not the offender, was to take responsibility for the cause of the incest. I have heard one professional testify that the offender does not even have to admit the abuse for him to "cure" him. He had, he said, treated and "cured" 60 sex offenders, not all of whom even admitted committing the offense.

It is this crucial issue of standards which O'Connell, Leberg, and Donaldson address, and they do so admirably. The sex offender treatment specialist will find that they have well represented the current state of the art. While not claiming that treatment specialists know more than we do, they do outline the most up-to-date knowledge available. This book will be one of the building blocks to developing adequate programs for sex offenders.

REFERENCES

Abel, G. G., Beck, J. V., Mittleman, M., Cunningham-Rathner, J., Rouleau, J. L., & Murphy, W. D. (1987). Self-reported sex crimes of nonincarcerated paraphilacs. *Journal of Interpersonal Violence, 2,* 3-25.

Abraham, K. (1927). The experiencing of sexual traumas as a form of sexual activity. In K. Abraham, *Selected papers* (pp. 47-62). London: Hogarth.

Hechler, D. (1987). *The battle and the backlash.* Lexington, MA: Lexington.

Herman, J. (1981). *Father-daughter incest.* Cambridge, MA: Harvard University Press.

Masson, J. M. (1984). *The assault on truth.* New York: Farrar, Straus & Giroux.

Mohr, J. W., Turner, R. E., & Jerry, M. B. (1964). *Pedophila and exhibitionism.* Toronto: University of Toronto Press.

Revitch, E., & Weiss, R. G. (1962). The pedophilac offender. *Diseases of the Nervous System, 33,* 73-79.

Rush, F. (1980). *The best kept secret: Sexual abuse of children.* New York: McGraw-Hill.

Russell, D. (1984). *Sexual exploitation: Rape, child abuse, and workplace harassment.* Beverly Hills, CA: Sage.

Salter, A. C. (1988). *Treating child sex offenders and victims: A practical guide.* Newbury Park, CA: Sage.

Slovenko, R. (1971). Statutory rape. *Medical Aspects of Human Sexuality, 5,* 155-167.

Virkkunen, M. (1976). Victim-precipitated pedophilia offenses. *British Journal of Criminology, 15*(2), 175-180.

Virkkunen, M. (1981). The child as participating victim. In M. Cook and K. Howells (Eds.), *Adult sexual interest in children* (pp. 121-134). New York: Academic.

Preface

Sex crimes have received growing attention over the past decade. Media attention and education in schools have resulted in greater numbers of reports of sexual abuse from a variety of sources. Victims themselves increasingly report having been sexually abused.

As a result of the increased reports of sexual abuse, criminal justice agencies have expanded resources to apprehend, prosecute, and punish sex offenders. Consequently, resources to incarcerate sex offenders have become strained. Additionally, there is a general perception that incarceration alone does not deter these offenders from committing new crimes on release.

The criminal justice system, especially the courts, receives pressure from a variety of sources to consider alternatives to prison. Although the general public holds the view that child molesters ought to be dealt with severely, when the offender is a friend, neighbor, or family member, this view tends to soften. Families and friends of offenders, many of whom may not believe the victim, have routinely lobbied against harsh sentences. Victims themselves often will petition the court to get help for offenders, perhaps not wanting to feel that offenders have gone to prison as a result of their having reported the offense. Judges' decisions are made even more difficult because many sex offenders appear to be different from the usual defendants seen in court. They tend, as a group, to have held long-term employment and to have been involved in the community in other productive ways, and they appear to be nonviolent and truly repentant for their actions. Finally, there is often a therapist in the picture who has conducted an evaluation and is optimistic about an individual offender's chances as a treatment candidate.

The decision to allow community-based treatment of sex offenders rests with the criminal justice system. This choice is not free from risk. Abel, Mittelman, Becker, Cunningham-Rathner, and Lucas (1983) and

Hindman (1988) suggested that sex offenders tend to have committed more types of sex offenses and had more victims than are known at the time of arrest. In addition, there is continuing debate within the therapeutic community over the methods that are most effective for the treatment of sexual deviancy. At the same time, we hear tragic examples of sex offenders who reoffend during, or shortly after, treatment. Some of these reoffenses are arguably traceable to therapist errors in judgment. Not all therapists have the basic training or experience to deal safely with this type of client.

The dilemma faced by the criminal justice system is how to go about selecting therapists and treatment programs that are mindful of the risks involved and that understand how best to minimize those risks. The research and writing in this field have tended to focus on offenders, victims, and treatment strategies for each. There has been little said about therapists and their approach to risk management with sex offenders.

The intent of this book is to suggest guidelines for the selection of therapists who provide sex offenders treatment in the community. This book is primarily designed to assist judges, prosecuting attorneys, child protection caseworkers, and probation and parole officers in identifying the issues that are key to deciding how to choose these therapists. Others, such as victim advocates or defense attorneys who may want a framework to help them decide how to refer an offender for evaluation or treatment, should also find this book of interest. Finally, this book may be helpful to the therapist who wants to decide whether or not to treat sex offenders.

We began this work by asking ourselves some fundamental questions: Why does this need to be done? By what authority can we presume to address this problem? What is the current state of the art for treatment of sex offenders? Has anyone else already developed guidelines for selecting sex offender therapists? We also asked ourselves: What is fair to the victim, what is fair to the offender, and what is fair to the therapist? We recognized the wide philosophical differences regarding the causes of and treatments for sexual deviancy.

We saw as the overriding concern the answer to the first question: Why does this need to be done? We need to set standards because offenders do such serious harm that evaluating and controlling them are extremely important. Evaluation and control are carried out in large part by the therapist.

A basic assumption we make is that the safety of the community should be the primary factor guiding all court decisions for sex offenders. The best way to make safety-related decisions is to be informed about the elements of risk represented by sex offenders. One of the potential risks that has received too little attention is how the therapist who works with sex offenders views this work.

No therapist who has worked with sex offenders for any length of time would ever *guarantee* a treated offender against reoffense. An experienced therapist tends to be even more skeptical about offenders just entering treatment. Nonetheless, there are some basic practices that an experienced therapist incorporates carefully into work with sex offenders that serve to reduce the risks involved. These practices lend themselves to most, if not all, treatment modalities.

As we began to review the literature on the subject in 1983, we did not discover any persuasive research demonstrating that one form of therapeutic approach was clearly more effective than another. This is an area that merits further research. We did uncover some research and writing pointing the way to successful avenues for evaluating and treating sex offenders that are generally harmonious with the concepts presented here (Abel et al., 1984; Dreiblatt, 1982; Salter, 1988). We encourage the reader to be alert to these and other new developments in the field. We have attempted to design a selection process that does not promote any one modality of treatment over another.

We discovered that, while there were no widely published guidelines for the evaluation and selection of therapists for sex offenders, there had been some local efforts to point out the key elements that sex offender evaluations should contain. We surveyed some 300 local and national experts, asking for comment on the need for criteria and on the criteria we proposed in the survey, and we received the clear message that standards were indeed needed and that our criteria were on the right track. More recently, Peters and McGovern have published general criteria by which offenders should be evaluated (Walker, 1987). Encouraged by this trend, we have attempted to produce guidelines that will be helpful to communities that are faced with the problems we encountered.

The final issue to be settled was what approach to use in the application of these guidelines. Some professionals suggested that we develop a list of approved therapists. We feel that the list approach is highly subject to personal bias and does not allow for the easy addition of new therapists. (If it *is* easy for new therapists to get on the list, there is little reason to have one in the first place.) Who gets on a given list may depend more on who keeps it than on the qualifications of the therapists. In the absence of any clearly stated criteria, the process would be a highly subjective one rather than a true test of ability.

Others thought that a licensing process was the answer, but the licensing approach is cumbersome and unlikely to be adopted by most jurisdictions. Legislation is generally needed to authorize an official reviewing body to carry out the licensing process. The process itself would need to be defined, including a clear statement of the criteria by which applicants would be judged, how prospective therapists would apply, and how they could respond to rejection of their applications. Funds would need to be appropriated for this purpose. Although some jurisdictions might enact the necessary legislation and programs, most would not.

After considerable debate, we chose a third alternative: providing guidelines local officials could use in the selection of sex offender therapists. These guidelines would assist in deciding which therapists should be recommended or approved. How then are these guidelines to be used effectively? Our intent is to write them for those officials and professionals who deal with these cases in the course of their daily work. Those in the social service and criminal justice fields are probably in the best position to make decisions about selecting therapists, provided they are well informed about how to identify therapists who are able to treat sexual deviancy and manage the risks.

Although such an alternative does not provide clear-cut answers, it does serve to focus debate on the issues of community safety and risk management in an outpatient treatment setting. This educational approach is an attempt to strike a middle ground between listing and licensing. We are not attempting to provide a recipe for making the correct choice because we cannot presume that conditions for dealing with sex offenders are identical in every locality. Our hope is to illuminate the important elements to be considered in the selection process so that those who face this problem will have a basis for reaching a sound decision.

The criteria set out in this book are, in a sense, a snapshot of conditions as they existed at the time it was written. We are still in an upward learning curve regarding our research and thinking about the evaluation and treatment of sex offenders. New methods and instruments are being developed, and our understanding of sex offenders is still far from complete. We consider this to be a work in progress, not a final answer. If we are able to stimulate discussion that leads to safer treatment of sex offenders, then we have achieved our goal.

Chapter One

Introduction

The purpose of this book is to outline a process by which community supervision agents, judges, prosecuting attorneys, probation and parole officers, and others can decide which therapists should be selected to treat sex offenders. We also discuss what should take place in the evaluation process and during the course of treatment for sexual deviancy. Our conclusions and recommendations are based on a number of assumptions we make about sex offenses and sex offenders. These lead us to some additional assumptions about what constitutes appropriate treatment, the qualifications necessary for therapists who would treat sex offenders, and the social context within which specialized treatment for sexual deviancy takes place. In this chapter we will outline and review those assumptions.

SEX OFFENSES

We define sexual offending as a criminal offense involving sexual behavior when one party does not give, or is incapable of giving, fully informed consent. This would include such situations as forcible rape and peeping or exposing where the victim obviously does not consent to be involved. It also includes situations where the difference in power between the two parties is such that one is not in a position to make a truly free choice. This would certainly be the case when one party is an adult and the other a child.

Sex offenses can be committed by both male and female offenders upon both male and female victims. However, the preponderance of

11

reported offenses involves male offenders and female or child victims (Finkelhor, 1982). For purposes of simplicity and brevity, we will refer to the generic sex offender as male and the generic victim as female.

Sex offenses are a problem for many reasons. The violation of the victim's person and integrity is a particularly damaging experience. Finkelhor and Browne (1985) have documented the enormous, long-term, and often life-altering and damaging effects of sexual abuse for the victim (see Chapter 2, "A Primer on Victimology"). The family of the victim is affected, too, as is the community at large, when they try to put the pieces back together. The cyclical nature of sexual abuse is dramatic. Many sexual abuse victims become sex offenders themselves, whereas others find themselves in family situations where the sexual abuse pattern is continued for additional generations, thus multiplying the effects of the original assault (Finkelhor & Browne, 1985; Groth, Burgess, Birnbaum, & Gary, 1978).

If any method of intervention is to be useful in preventing further victimization and the problems that sex offending creates, there should be some thought given to what causes the behavior in the first place. We believe that some sense can be made of this behavior. Understanding and dealing with offending behavior from this standpoint will make it more likely that reoffense and further victimization can be substantially reduced. It seems to us that sex offending behavior is driven by a combination of factors:

(1) attraction to the behavior because of the pleasure derived,
(2) a perception that there are no other available means of obtaining pleasure,
(3) a lack of concern or understanding about the damage that results from this behavior, and
(4) insufficient controls to prevent the offender from acting on a desire to seek pleasure in this way.

It may seem absurdly simplistic to say that sex offenders act the way they do because they like it, but keeping that in mind will be helpful in avoiding some of the confusion about this behavior and the issues surrounding it. Sex offenders commit sex offenses because it makes them feel good, at least momentarily. Pursuing pleasure in this way may be, in part, an escape from other painful or unpleasant circumstances. There may be some unpleasant consequences of this behavior for offenders, such as fear, shame, and so on. However, when a sex offense occurs it is because, at that moment, the pleasure derived from the behavior overrides all other considerations. There are a variety of theories about how this behavior becomes so pleasurable for some people, and the understanding of the process of how this occurs is incomplete. We will not attempt, here, to make a definitive explanation of sexual deviancy. Nevertheless, it is important to realize that sex offenses are committed in the process of seeking pleasure.

Sometimes offenders simply have a strong preference for a particular type of pleasure seeking that happens to involve victimizing others. Often, however, offenders feel themselves to be faced with limited choices; they see few ways to glean a meager bit of comfort in what they perceive as an unrelentingly hostile world. In either case, offenders usually have some understanding that the sex offending behavior is wrong or could get them in trouble (offenses are generally done in secret). They do not, however, have a strong enough reason *not* to offend when compared with the perceived pleasure to be derived. There are not enough controls, either internal (recognition of the harm to victim, wanting to do the right thing, and so on) or external (fear of getting caught, concern about what others would think if they knew, and so on). Offenders have some combination of overpowering attraction to the behavior (compulsivity) or lack of control (impulsivity).

SEX OFFENDERS

Sex offenders are different from most psychotherapy clients. Most people who are in a counseling relationship go into that situation on their own initiative to solve problems that are causing them concern and that they are more or less committed to facing and resolving. On the other hand, most sex offenders go into treatment involuntarily. Substantial outside pressure must be applied to motivate them to deal with these issues. That is not to say that offenders have never been in counseling before; often they have, but usually dealing with other tangential and less difficult issues. It is rare for offenders to bring up, on their own, the issue of their sex offending. On the rare occasions when that does occur, offenders are usually not willing to follow through with the commitment necessary to bring about the changes required to prevent reoffense or further victimization.

No matter how attractive the offending behavior may be to offenders, in order to commit the first offense they had to cross substantial legal, social, and ethical boundaries. For most people, those boundaries and controls are so clear and powerful that no serious thought is given to crossing them. That explains why most people react with some combination of shock, horror, and incomprehension when considering the issue of sexual victimization. For some reason, offenders either don't have those controls operating in their lives or, in some way, they have managed to avoid them. When offenders begin to avoid those boundaries, it may be with forethought and full knowledge that they intend to do significant damage to another, vulnerable human being. Usually this is not the case. Commonly, the process of giving themselves permission to engage in this sort of behavior takes place subtly, imperceptibly, and gradually over time.

Another way in which sex offenders are different from many other psychotherapy clients is that their problems are much more severe than first appearances would suggest. Offenders usually do not see themselves as callous and hurtful because they maintain many of the trappings of prosocial concern and respectability. They fool themselves and those around them: They do not see themselves as sex offenders and they may not appear to others as sex offenders. In fact, they are most likely to look pretty "normal" (Abel et al., 1983). Typically, they cannot deal openly and honestly with who they are or what they have done. This is not surprising: With something to hide, they have become practiced at hiding it, often (in part) from themselves as well as from others. Offenders are not truthful about the full nature and extent of their sexual deviancy and other kinds of hurtful and antisocial behavior. The truth, when it becomes known, inevitably involves more incidents of abuse and, often, different types of deviancy than those originally reported (American Psychiatric Association, 1987, p. 280). Often, additional victims are discovered (Abel et al., 1983).

Another way in which sex offenders are different from other psychotherapy clients is that they tend to be unrealistically optimistic about their ability to control their behavior and to prevent reoffense from occurring. They come to treatment as a result of an inability to control their behavior in a responsible way. They have demonstrated that they are not good predictors of their own behavior. A typical part of the sex offense cycle is for offenders to promise themselves to refrain from any further offense behavior and to believe that they can make this resolve stick. Abel, Mittelman, and Becker (1985) reported that, in spite of this, the offender is likely to return to offending. There may be a hiatus, sometimes for years or decades. For example, in cases of intrafamilial child sexual abuse (incest of daughter, stepchild, and so on), the abuse may be brought to the attention of the nonoffending parent or community authorities, and the offending will cease for a time. The fear of criminal consequences, or just the social ostracism and embarrassment, may provide a sufficient deterrent. Often, however, reoffense will occur some time later, after the sting of being confronted has faded into memory and the old sexual arousal patterns return. Thus sex offenders cannot be regarded as good predictors of the effectiveness of therapy, as can many other psychotherapy clients.

TREATMENT OF SEX OFFENDERS

Having made some sense of how and why the sex offense behavior occurs and recognizing that sex offenders have some unique qualities lead us to the question of what to do when a sex offense comes to public and official attention. We make an assumption that the main purpose of intervention is to prevent further victimization. To accomplish this, *sufficient external controls must be imposed* to prevent reoffense and other more subtle forms of victimization while working with offenders to (a) reduce attraction to offense behavior; (b) develop appropriate social, emotional, and behavioral alternatives to deviant sexuality as a means of seeking pleasure; and (c) develop necessary social, behavioral, and internal controls. *Substantial external controls should be maintained until these steps are accomplished and tested.*

For the purposes of this book, we will be looking at how this can be accomplished in an outpatient, community-based setting. We make a major assumption that community safety and prevention of further victimization are the primary goals of any attempt at treatment. We recognize that some offenders cannot be dealt with under the guidelines we have developed because they cannot be safely treated in the community. They should be evaluated and treated in a more secure setting. The initial evaluation process should be sufficiently rigorous to distinguish such offenders from those for whom community-based treatment is a viable option. (The evaluation process is discussed in greater detail in Chapter 5.)

It is essential that the therapist treating sex offenders knows the full nature, extent, and history of sexual deviancy so that (a) a clear and complete definition of the problem can be made; (b) sufficient controls can be imposed; (c) appropriate methods can be applied to deal with the problem; and (d) the potential for reoffense (highly likely without appropriate controls and treatment intervention) can be minimized.

Offenders cannot be counted on to give a complete and accurate account of their antisocial history. The therapist evaluating and treating offenders must have access to information from other parties involved in these cases. From this it is clear that effective treatment of sex offenders cannot take place in isolation without corroborating information and the

active support of community supervision agents. This requires a clear and open line of communication between the therapist treating the offender and other actors in the drama that sexual abuse creates. Thus confidentiality, in the sense that it applies in most voluntary treatment situations, is not appropriate in the treatment of sex offenders.

The reason for confidentiality in traditional therapy is to give clients a sense of confidence that what is told to the therapist will not be used to hurt them, allowing them to open up and develop a trusting relationship with the therapist. With or without confidential communication, sex offenders will not be inclined to be open and honest with anyone about their sexual deviancy. Thus the evaluating and treating therapist must have more than just the offender's description of the presenting problem.

For a full and complete understanding of the nature and extent of deviant and antisocial history, the therapist should have access to the following:

(1) complete official case records, including police reports, victim statements, and so on, and other relevant information as it becomes known to officials involved in the case;

(2) officials involved in supervising the case and the offender;

(3) the victim or the victim's therapist, to become familiar with the impact of the offense upon the victim;

(4) other significant persons in the offender's life, such as spouse and family members;

(5) physiological testing, including polygraph and penile plethysmograph, to compare with offender's self-report of behavior and sexual arousal patterns.

It is only with this complete array of information that a therapist can be expected to begin to understand the sex offender client, what controls need to be imposed, and what sort of treatment interventions are likely to be useful in making the necessary changes.

THERAPISTS TREATING SEX OFFENDERS

Our experience is that not every therapist is qualified to undertake this work, and, when offenders are treated by those without the necessary skills, the likelihood of reoffense increases to an unacceptable level. Most psychotherapists who provide treatment services in an outpatient setting are not, in the normal course of their practice, prepared to deal with some of the most important issues that are present when working with sex offenders. This is because, as noted above, offenders are different from most other clients a therapist is likely to see in a general practice. Likewise, the nature of treatment for offenders should be quite different from what takes place in most outpatient therapy. Thus the therapist who treats sex offenders must have some specific and uncommon qualifications, experiences, and personal qualities to do an effective job of reducing the likelihood of reoffense. We describe those qualifications in some detail in Chapter 4.

COMMUNITY CONTEXT

The way in which most offenders come to therapy is quite different from the self-referred situation. It is usually the community that is saying, in effect, "This is a serious problem that needs fixing." Offenders commonly take the position that there is no real problem, or, if there had been, it has now been resolved. The result of this unique situation is that in a significant way the community is the therapist's client at least as much as the offender. This is a very different situation for therapists whose training and practice have generally prepared them to see their professional and ethical responsibility as being primarily to the individual, not the community.

Because the community has a stake in the outcome, it has a legitimate right to know that evaluation and treatment are being conducted in a way that has a reasonable chance of accomplishing the primary purpose of preventing further victimization. *The therapist who treats a sex offender in a community-based setting must consider that what he or she is doing is making a tacit statement that the offender is safe to be at large and that treatment has a reasonable chance of reducing the likelihood of reoffense.* The people and agencies making judgments about the legal disposition, the protection of the community, and the supervision of offenders should know that evaluation and treatment decisions are made by a knowledgeable, experienced professional who takes due care to minimize the risk of further victimization. Thus the therapist should be expected to share information about evaluation and treatment of a particular sex offender that includes the following:

(1) what has been included in the evaluation and treatment process, what is expected of the offender, and what means are to be used to determine effective completion of treatment;

(2) relevant, specific issues dealt with and problems encountered in dealing with this offender; and

(3) any infractions or indications of possible or actual reoffense.

In effect, this involves the therapist as an integral part of a system of community supervision and behavioral control. This is, again, very different from the typical outpatient therapy situation and requires the therapist to be more than just the offender's professional agent who helps the offender work on issues that he defines. In fact, offenders will often see the therapist as an adversary who challenges their perceptions of the meaning of the offending behavior and who is part of a team that imposes and maintains external controls. For a therapist to distrust the self-report of a client, to go to such extremes as using a lie detector to check the truthfulness of the client's report, and then to tell the authorities if something is amiss is a very different kind of counseling relationship indeed. It requires that the therapist make judgments about whether a particular offender is a good risk to be at large, to live in a setting where there are past or potential victims, and so on. If the therapist thinks that there is a risk, it must be communicated to the appropriate authorities (consistent with the legal ability to do so), even when the offender does not agree with that assessment. Offenders are likely to find this sort of situation intrusive, invading those areas of personal and family life that most of us prefer to keep private. But privacy, or secrecy, is the atmosphere within which offending takes place. If the primary concern in these extraordinary situations involving sexually abusive and exploitive behavior is to prevent reoffense, we believe that these kinds of intrusions into the private lives of offenders are necessary and justified.

Because this sort of therapy situation is so different from what one expects when hiring the services of a psychotherapist, offenders entering treatment or being evaluated must be provided with the information they need to make an informed decision to participate in such a program. It is also reasonable, especially because so much is at stake in these situations, for offenders to have the opportunity to get a second professional opinion about these matters. However, this should not be the first step in a shopping-for-a-therapist procedure or a tactic to avoid being called to account for offending by delaying legal proceedings.

What we have attempted to do in this introduction is to outline some basic assumptions we have about community-based evaluation and treatment of sex offenders. Assuming that the primary purpose of such treatment is to protect the safety of the community and to prevent reoffense, it seems reasonable that the community, through its justice and community protection agencies, should exercise some oversight to ensure that what takes place in treatment is likely to meet that primary purpose. The community has an interest in knowing whether a therapist working with sex offenders is willing and able to deal with the various, necessary issues. Because criminal justice disposition in these cases is often based on the recommendation of a therapist that a particular offender is a good risk for community-based treatment, the community has a right to know how and with what sources of information that determination was made.

The purpose of this book is to provide some fairly objective, understandable criteria with which to decide if the community's interest in preventing further offending is being adequately addressed by a particular therapist or treatment program. The chapters that follow discuss the basic issues of victimology, the necessary basic professional qualifications of a therapist treating sex offenders, what should be included in an initial evaluation report, and what should take place in treatment. A quality-control process is necessary because most therapists are not knowledgeable or experienced in working with the special issues of sexual deviancy. Offenders have, at best, mixed feelings about giving up access to a source of pleasure that has, as they perceive it, served them well. They also fear the consequences of full disclosure of their history of sexual deviancy. They are not likely on their own to choose a treatment program that will include the elements necessary to truly reduce the risks of reoffense. Someone else needs to make those quality-control decisions. We believe that following the steps outlined here will make it possible to make that decision in a more thorough, well-informed, and objective way. We foresee this outline of criteria being useful to sentencing judges, prosecuting and defense attorneys, probation and parole officers, victim advocates, and therapists wanting to decide whether to treat sex offenders.

Before beginning to discuss the specific recommendations of what should be included in the evaluation and treatment of sex offenders, we would like to make a few cautionary remarks. First, this book limits its scope to adult offenders who have committed sex offenses involving a limited amount of violence. Juvenile offenders, although they may need to deal with many of the same issues as do adult offenders, are sufficiently different that we will not address their needs here. In addition, there are two groups of adult sex offenders whose treatment will not be addressed here: (1) rapists, violent offenders, and those with insufficient personal and social supports to safely and successfully participate in a community-based program, and (2) those whose deviant behaviors are so ingrained as to require especially intensive treatment. Such offenders require an inpatient, institutional treatment program. Further, it is the belief of the authors that for some offenders present knowledge limitations are such that no available treatment methods can provide the necessary assurance of community safety from reoffense. In those cases, the only responsible option is to remove them from opportunities to reoffend with long-term institutional confinement.

It should be remembered that definitive knowledge about what works in the treatment of sex offenders is limited. We are operating on the frontier of understanding how to make sense of deviant sexuality and how to effect change in offenders so they do not return to such exploitive behavior. We do not attempt to endorse any particular modality of treatment. Instead, we strive to synthesize what professionals who specialize in such therapy have generally agreed on as the essential elements of treatment. Finally, we outline the safeguards that should be in place so that, in both the short and long run, risk of reoffense and danger to the community can be minimized.

Chapter Two

A Primer on Victimology

In order to understand this approach to dealing with sex offenders, it is important that the reader and the therapist evaluating or treating the offender understand what it means to be a victim of sexual abuse. Because the majority of offenders who will be considered for treatment in a community setting will have offended against children, this primer on victimology addresses the child who has been sexually abused by an adult. The following is a primer, not a definitive discussion. Browne and Finkelhor's (1986) review of the research literature provides more detailed information on the impact of child sexual abuse. Although various combinations of people can be involved, we will be using as examples generic situations with female child victims and father-figure offenders.

The circumstances in which adults have sex with children tend to protect the adults while leaving the victims relatively defenseless. The fact that sexual exploitation of children takes place in secret provides cover for offenders. Alone with offenders, victims are usually in a position where they are expected to follow the directives of the adult. Offenders are in the position of defining the experience. For example, sexual abuse can be presented to children as a demonstration of love or sharing a special secret. Children are not able to give their informed consent to participate in such behavior because they are not capable of understanding the implications of what is going to happen. Given their intellectual, social, and emotional development, children cannot comprehend adult sexual behavior, much less understand the long-term consequences of being used as an object for sexual enjoyment.

Although some children clearly refuse to be sexual with adults, others are often unable to effectively resist the sexual advances of adults, especially parent figures. The advantages enjoyed by adults in terms of knowledge, physical size, and authority make it extremely difficult for children to repel the abuse.

Community agencies and the criminal justice system are mobilized when a child is sexually exploited by an adult, not because the abuser has offended some rule of polite behavior, but because he has caused significant harm to a particularly vulnerable victim. We will explore here the harm to victims of sexual abuse. Finkelhor and Browne (1985) reported that the damage experienced by victims may include traumatic sexualization, stigmatization, betrayal, and powerlessness. Following a discussion of those factors, we will explore some aspects of victimization that, if not understood, may make it difficult to accept victims' reports of abuse. These aspects include children's accommodation to the abuse, delayed and unconvincing disclosure, and retraction.

TRAUMATIC SEXUALIZATION

The most obvious result of sexual abuse is that children's sexuality may be shaped in a way that is inappropriate to their age and level of development. This often results in both emotional and behavioral problems. Problems can develop either from children becoming fixated on the premature sexualization or from the experience being so aversive as to impair their ability to function in appropriate and satisfying ways as they grow older.

Fixated or precocious sexualization results from victims being rewarded (often with special attention or affection) for inappropriate sexual behavior. For offenders, the fantasy that typically accompanies the abuse is that the child "loves it." The more the child fulfills this fantasy, the more pleasurable is the experience for the offender. The more pleasure the adult experiences, the more the child is likely to be rewarded. In this process, parts of the child's body become fetishized and are given distorted importance. This disrupts children's normal sexual development. The result is that victims confuse sex with love and caring. They learn that the way to obtain approval and attention is to be sexual, and they may develop uncertainty about what is appropriate sexual behavior. Child victims may engage in sexually precocious and obsessive behavior (Friedrich, Urquiza, & Beilke, in press; Tufts' New England Medical Center, 1984). Many sexual abuse victims become sexually promiscuous.

A high percentage of prostitutes were former sexual abuse victims (James & Meyerding, 1977; Silbert & Pines, 1981). Former victims are ill equipped as parents to model appropriate sexual boundaries or to provide their children with protection against sexual exploitation.

On the other hand, for many victims the abuse experience pairs sexual activity with negative emotions and memories. This results in negative or phobic feelings about their bodies and about sexuality in general. This can lead to avoidance of intimacy and sexuality in adult relationships or to sexual dysfunction (Herman, 1981; Langmade, 1983; Meiselman, 1978).

STIGMATIZATION

Feelings of guilt and shame for having been sexually abused often become part of sexual abuse victims' self-image (Bagley & Ramsay, 1985; Courtois, 1979). Even very young children know that there must be something bad about the sexual activity because it has to be kept secret. The way in which the instructions to keep the secret are presented often makes this sense of badness even greater. Victims may be told that, if they tell, "I won't love you any more," "you'll be hurting your mother," "it will break up the family," or "you'll get me in trouble." However, everything will be all right if they just "don't tell." But, by not telling, children become co-conspirators and are made to feel responsible for the abuse occurring in the first place.

As a result, victims may be left with feelings of worthlessness: feeling like spoiled goods. They often have a strong and unpleasant sense of being different from others. Because they feel less worthy than others, child victims will often want to be alone, to isolate themselves (Briere, 1984). A powerfully attractive way to isolate oneself from others is to escape through alcohol and drugs. Another, more direct way is to run away from home. Feeling that they have no value, victims may act out, confirming their image of worthlessness through prostitution or other criminal activity. They may engage in self-destructive behavior such as self-mutilation or suicide attempts.

Unfortunately, there is no easy escape from this feeling of worthlessness. If the child discloses the abuse, the reaction of the offender, and often many others, is one of shock, horror, and hysteria, and they blame the victim. Some may change their attitude toward the victim, communicating in direct or in subtle, unconscious ways that they believe her to have diminished value as a person.

BETRAYAL

Sexual abuse victims often feel betrayed because someone, on whom they were vitally dependent, has caused them significant harm. This sense of betrayal can come from several different sources. First of all, the offender has taken advantage of the child's trust and vulnerability. In pursuing his personal pleasure, the abuser has disregarded his responsibility to consider the welfare of the child. But the victims can feel betrayed by others, also. The child may feel that family members or others were unable or, worse, unwilling to protect her from the abuse. Or they may fail to believe the child when she discloses abuse.

As a result, the victims often experience a feeling of abandonment. Sometimes this is expressed by children exhibiting clinging behavior. Younger victims, especially, may physically hang on to whoever seems to be available to offer them comfort. Needing some redeeming relationship to compensate for the betrayal leads some victims to indiscriminate or desperate emotional attachment to others. Victims thus become vulnerable to further sexual, physical, or emotional abuse (Briere, 1984; Miller et al., 1978; Russell, in press). When victims become adults, they may not be able to sever relationships in which both they and their children are being abused.

Whereas some victims respond to this betrayal as abandonment, others experience a generalized sense of disillusionment and detachment. They avoid any kind of intimate relationship, which leads to emotional and social isolation (Briere, 1984; Courtois, 1979). Some victims express this disillusionment in anger. Especially among adolescents, this anger can be acted out in antisocial ways. Angry striking out seems to act as a way of protecting themselves against further hurt and betrayal.

POWERLESSNESS

The final major consequence to victims of sexual abuse to be discussed here is the feeling of powerlessness. This results from the experience of their body being violated. Not only are victims unable to prevent this violation, but often the abuse is repeated over and over, reinforcing this sense of helplessness. Feeling unable to protect themselves can cause chronic anxiety and fear (Tufts' New England Medical Center, 1984). This can be manifested in a variety of symptoms, such as nightmares, phobias, and physical complaints.

Feeling unable to manage and cope with life's problems and challenges can leave sexual abuse victims at high risk of further victimization. Victims can carry these feelings of helplessness throughout their lives. Even as adults, former victims can feel powerless to protect themselves from others who try to manipulate them or do them harm. Alternatively, some victims try to gain a feeling of control by becoming bullies or offenders. This reenactment of their own abuse finally places them in the position of power. In neither case, however, do victims gain a true sense of personal power or self-sufficiency.

Having looked at the harm done to victims of sexual abuse, we will now explore some aspects of victimization that make it difficult to accept the victim's report. As shown above, victims of sexual abuse are subject to a devastating array of hurt and damage. Rational, responsible people often find it difficult to believe that friends, neighbors, people like themselves, are capable of inflicting such pain on another human being. The idea that an adult can achieve substantial pleasure from sexual involvement with a child seems incredible to most of us. When a child discloses sexual abuse, the natural inclination is not to believe it could be possible.

In such cases, an attempt is made to explain how such an allegation could have been made, often by perceiving the victim as precociously sexual and seductive, or as vindictive and untrustworthy. Several aspects of child sexual abuse feed into these faulty attempts to make sense of a report of sexual exploitation. Summit (1983) reported that these include the child's accommodation to the abuse, delayed and unconvincing disclosure, and a tendency for victims to retract their report of abuse.

CHILD'S ACCOMMODATION TO THE ABUSE

Most people generally assume that victims of sexual assault would fight off an attacker with all they had at their disposal. For child victims especially, the circumstances under which such assaults take place make this nearly impossible. Sometimes the nature of the relationship between offenders and victims makes it difficult for children to even know that abuse is occurring. Sexual assaults on children frequently entail a lengthy grooming phase where the lines between appropriate physical contact and contact of a sexual nature become blurred. In the absence of clear information about appropriate versus inappropriate touching, it may be some time before children are aware that anything is wrong or associate the discomfort they feel with the sexual content of the touching. By this time, well-groomed children will have learned to mistrust their own perceptions of right and wrong and may well have learned the futility of challenging adult authority. Thus a typical response on the part of children in attempting to avoid the abuse is to play possum by feigning sleep and rolling over or pulling up the covers. By virtue of the fact that they are children, they cannot normally use force as a means of dealing with the sexual assault. Offenders, whose fantasy usually involves the distorted conception that their victims enjoy the sexual contact, discount these signs of resistance. We usually don't see children resisting forcefully until the sexual abuse is quite advanced, they have gotten old enough (and strong enough) to feel that resistance may work, or they have become convinced that there is no other measure left to stop the assaults.

Given the fact that victims are really unable to prevent the abuse, they may come to believe that they are in some way responsible for the painful encounters. They may attempt to make up for their badness by trying to earn love and acceptance and become good or worthy. Within the context of the abuse situation, with the offender being someone the victim is dependent on, the way to be a good kid is to accommodate the offender's desire for sexual interaction and, more important, keep the secret as instructed. This accommodation technique needs to be seen for what it is, a way for children to survive the abuse. It does not mitigate the offenders' responsibility or justify their behavior.

DELAYED AND UNCONVINCING DISCLOSURE

When abuse does get reported, there are several rationales used to question the credibility of children's disclosures.

(1) It has often been a long time since the abuse started. Without understanding the accommodation syndrome described above, many people tend to discount reports made so long after the fact.

(2) The children may look too well. There may be no outward signs of abuse occurring. In fact, children may have successfully accommodated to the abuse and learned how to appear normal, often while secretly experiencing many of the traumatic effects described earlier.

(3) Other victims lose credibility by being unsuccessful at accommodating the abuse. They develop histories of acting-out behavior and acquire reputations for being untrustworthy, or they seem to have asked for the sexual encounters by being sexually provocative.

In fact, many of these attributes are likely to be the direct result of being abused. In cases of long-term abuse that began when the child was quite young, disclosure may not take place until the victim becomes old enough and feels strong enough to engage the abuser in an emotional struggle. This often takes place when the child is at the stage of development where adolescent limit testing occurs. However, this also provides the offender with a plausible explanation for the child's disclosure: "The kid has been acting out." The parent has been attempting to enforce rules and boundaries of acceptable behavior. The child is accused of making up allegations of sexual abuse as part of a power struggle with the parent. Most adults can identify with the parent who seems to be locked into such a battle with a rebellious child much more easily than they can comprehend the prospect of sexual abuse.

Sometimes, the victim's report of the details of the abuse seems to dribble out over time. This can lead to a perception that the child is making up the story as she goes along, or that she is being influenced to tell a more gruesome tale by a witch-hunting investigator. In fact, however, most victims tend not to report the full extent of the abuse. If they receive support and encouragement, they may disclose more over time.

RETRACTION

Victims often do not get support when they report the abuse. People tend to get terribly upset and often do not believe their reports. When this happens, victims tend to retract whatever they have reported. Victims often find that their worst fears come true: The offender denies the report of abuse and calls the victim a liar, others don't believe the victim, and the family is disrupted and publicly disgraced. It seems like things were better when the victim only had the abuse to contend with; so the victim may solve this mess by retracting the report of the abuse and saying that she made up a story about being molested. This fits in with what others would really rather believe, and things seem to settle down.

In fact, the vast preponderance of such reports of sexual abuse are true. This is validated in situations where there is special support for child victims along with official intervention (Wheeler, 1987). This intervention should include specialized evaluation and treatment of the offender in keeping with the recommendations outlined in the following chapters. When this is available, not only do victims feel less pressure to retract, but a substantial number of abusers end up acknowledging the truthfulness of the victims' reports. In fact, offenders in treatment often report additional abuse that children do not disclose.

In summary, the sexual abuse of children is characterized by secrecy and by the victims being in a position of physical and emotional powerlessness. When (and if) abuse is reported, there is a tendency for others not to believe that it could have occurred. This is because of a variety of social forces and pressures to doubt victims' reports. However, sexual abuse of children occurs more often than most of us want to believe. When it does occur, sexual abuse causes substantial and often long-term problems for the victims. These problems for victims stem from feelings of powerlessness, betrayal, stigmatization, and traumatic sexualization.

Because sexual abuse is so damaging to victims, communities and official agencies must intervene. Community-based evaluation and treatment of sex offenders can be an integral part of that intervention. Effective evaluation and treatment of offenders need to be conducted in an environment where this basic information on victimology is understood. This understanding forms a basis for many of the recommendations presented in the following chapters. Appropriate intervention can play an important role in reducing the likelihood of reoffense. Preventing reoffense and limiting the damage caused to victims by offering support and providing physical and emotional safety are goals of the highest order.

Chapter Three

Gathering Information About Therapists

Before we discuss therapist qualifications, it may be helpful to spend some time discussing ways to gather information about a therapist who is being considered as a treater of sex offenders. In this chapter we present methods for gathering information. The chapters that follow dealing with therapist qualifications, evaluations, and treatment issues provide a framework within which to ask specific questions.

We suggest four methods for gathering information about a therapist:

(1) requesting written information
(2) interviewing the therapist
(3) observing the therapist's work
(4) checking references

It is important to be thorough in an evaluation of the therapist who will be treating sex offenders, especially when offenders remain at large in the community during treatment. Without doing all the hard work necessary to evaluate sex offenders, no therapist can make representations that a given offender does not represent a continuing, immediate danger to the community. By the same token, if representatives of the community who are entrusted to control sex offenders are not equally rigorous in the evaluation of a therapist to whom sex offenders are referred, those representatives are in no better position to guarantee the community's safety.

REQUESTING WRITTEN INFORMATION

There are some time-saving methods that may be employed in the information-gathering process. One of these involves requesting written information. Most therapists have put together a résumé of their academic and professional experiences. The relative value of this information is discussed in more detail in Chapter 4, "Therapist Qualifications." We view written information as a starting point from which to prepare for interviewing therapists.

Résumés are typically broken into several areas, including academic history, work experience, professional attainments, and other achievements. Academic history may be extensive but it is not the primary consideration for selecting a sex offender therapist. Education is best viewed as providing the framework for work experience and specialized professional training; it does not stand alone to qualify any person to treat sex offenders. Thus it may require some probing to find out where a given therapist learned how to evaluate and treat sex offenders.

A few therapists will have begun to practice in this special area many years ago. They will have developed their expertise through observation, trial and error, and careful evaluations of their work with sex offenders. They may also have collaborated with other therapists who work with offenders, victims, or nonoffending family members. Most therapists, however, will have learned their skills through consultation or collaboration with an experienced and recognized therapist in this field. This may have occurred in private practice or in a public hospital or clinical setting. Pay special attention to such information on the résumé. It may be necessary to establish that the therapist doing the training had the expertise to provide quality instruction.

Questionnaires or surveys are another method for gathering written information about a therapist. This is a relatively simple way for a reviewer to gather information about a number of therapists in a short period of time. It has the added benefit of providing a uniform approach to gathering information about a new therapist. It also provides information about which therapists will accept sex offenders as clients and allows the cataloguing of therapists as to availability, specialty, price, area served, or any other category that makes sense for the community.

The drawback to using questionnaires is that, unless they are brief, many therapists will not take the time to fill them out, including those therapists who might be good resources. But a brief questionnaire may be a superficial one that does not get at some of the more critical questions about how the therapist views confidentiality, community safety, and successful treatment.

Therapeutic assignments, writing projects for offenders, and offender self-evaluations are other forms of written material that may be helpful in understanding the work a therapist does. These materials may show how therapists get at some of the issues that must be dealt with in treatment. More thorough and demanding assignments may indicate that what goes on in treatment is more thorough and demanding as well.

INTERVIEWING THE THERAPIST

Interviewing the therapist is helpful, especially if the therapist is new to the area or just beginning to practice. The goal in the interview is the same as that for gathering written information: to review the background and treatment orientation the therapist brings to the practice. An interview gives more opportunity for a free-flowing information exchange. The interviewer has the opportunity to make the therapist aware of local expectations and to correct any misinformation the therapist may have about how offenders are handled. Thus the therapist can receive an orientation to a particular system. The interviewer needs to be clear and well focused on local needs and practices in order to gather as well as to provide information.

When interviewing, it is helpful to have a clear format in mind for the information to be gathered. Areas to address include (a) where the therapist learned to treat sex offenders, (b) the quantity and quality of experiences, (c) how the evaluation is conducted and what the report contains, and (d) treatment methods used by the therapist.

A review of the chapters on victims, therapist qualifications, evaluations, treatment, and family reunification will provide more specific information on issues that are important to explore.

OBSERVING THE THERAPIST'S WORK

It is not possible to determine how well a therapist evaluates and treats sex offenders by simply talking to or reading about the therapist. A better test is to observe examples of a therapist's work. Review of preliminary and final evaluations, progress reports, treatment plans, termination reports, and professional papers written or presented will provide a better idea of the quality of work that may be expected. When reviewing this material, it is possible to identify gaps in information, conclusions that do not follow from information presented, a particular bias or naïveté on the part of the therapist, inadequate safeguards or behavioral restrictions placed on the offender, and how the therapist views and handles the issue of community safety.

It is reasonable to expect that the therapist will provide examples of the best materials produced. The quality of this material will set the standard by which future work may be judged. Where possible, it is more useful to ask for the names of other professionals with whom the therapist has worked in the past and obtain a release to talk with them for the purposes of reviewing the quality of the therapist's work as they saw it. If this is not possible, it is still worthwhile to take a look at the materials the therapist supplies. An interviewer will be able to see how the therapist approaches the work, how it is organized and presented, and the steps the therapist has gone through to arrive at the completed work product. Questions raised at this stage should be discussed with the therapist, either in writing or in person.

As will be discussed in Chapter 5, reviewing the evaluation report is perhaps the easiest way to determine who should and should not treat sex offenders. A quality evaluation report will illustrate, as clearly as the therapist is able, the approach taken to working with sex offenders. Clarity, thoroughness, beliefs about sex offenders, confrontiveness, diligence, and concern for community safety are all generally made clear in the evaluation report.

There are some other ways to observe the therapist's work. Interviewing former clients to determine what they got out of therapy, how their lives have changed, and how they presently view their sexual deviancy is one method. Observing current clients over time to see how their thoughts about their deviancy and their behaviors have changed is another. Attending individual and group therapy sessions is a third. These methods all take time, but are generally well worth the effort as they provide a better feel for what is going on in treatment.

Other areas to observe include how the therapist handles issues of confidentiality, testifies in the courtroom setting, or demonstrates a working knowledge of the uses and limitations of the polygraph and plethysmograph. Observing the therapist's knowledge of and policies on the use of other community resources for service to clients may also help to determine qualifications. As offenders often come from situations where they have molested a child in their own household, observing how the therapist works with other professionals who might be involved with the family helps a reviewer understand how the therapist views his or her role in the treatment process. Finally, all of the materials gathered and observed above should be reviewed for evidence that this therapist is willing to put in the extra effort that these cases seem to require.

CHECKING REFERENCES

A final and very important aspect of gathering information about a therapist is checking references. We have suggested above some ways that this might be done. It is important that therapists who wish to treat sex offenders in the community allow a reviewer access to background information about themselves.

For those who have a widely known reputation for high-quality work, this may not be as critical a part of the process. It is essential when considering previously unknown therapists. Therapists should be able to provide the names of former colleagues, places of employment, academic institutions attended, and copies of certificates and awards received. It is good practice to obtain a release and verify these references. While the chance that this will turn up a fraudulent therapist is slight, it is worth the relatively small amount of time required to phone or write for verification. It is more likely that a reviewer will discover that qualifications have been either somewhat overstated or given more weight than intended. The reviewer may find that additional information about course work, work-shops, publications, and so on, which therapists might feel was not significant, may lead to a better assessment of a therapist's capabilities.

SUMMARY

Selection of therapists who will be treating sex offenders in a community setting requires careful work. The goal, at least for the community, is to be as certain as possible that the therapist treating sex offenders will be mindful of community safety and will not take undue risks by agreeing to treat offenders who pose a clear danger of reoffense. Those who must review and select, thereby sanctioning the work of therapists, owe the community just as much care in this process as the reviewer would expect from the therapist.

Chapter Four

Therapist Qualifications

Selection of a therapist to conduct evaluations and treatment of sex offenders is an important task. There are many areas to consider, not the least of which is the interest the community has in the eventual outcome of therapy. In Chapter 3 we discussed ways to gather information about a therapist. In this chapter, we will outline factors that should be considered regarding a therapist's qualifications. We will then move on to the more specific and detailed issues surrounding evaluations and treatment in the following chapters.

Several areas need to be covered in deciding whether a therapist should be selected to treat sex offenders. These include academic history, clinical experience, specialized knowledge, and some personal skills and qualities. While there may be information of value to therapists who read this work, this section is primarily intended for the reader who is placed in the position of recommending or approving a given therapist. Prosecuting attorneys, judges, and probation officers are normally given this responsibility, but police and children's protective workers may also be called on for a referral.

ACADEMIC QUALIFICATIONS

Formal educational training provides the basis upon which to build specialized knowledge. It provides the framework to integrate clinical experiences into work with this client population. This is also the area where it will be the easiest to gather information.

There are, at the time of this writing, no academic programs within the United States that are specifically designed to teach specialized therapy for sex offenders. Thus any academic work done is only a *base* for learning how to treat sex offenders. Education is, however, an important component of any therapist's background and should not be overlooked. Undergraduate and graduate course work provides the building blocks upon which a therapist establishes a clinical practice. The therapist should have a solid grasp of personality development, cognitive development and processes, social skills development, learning theory, and the like. As described in greater detail in Chapter 5, the therapist who treats sex offenders must possess the skills to assess a wide range of behaviors and describe them in a sensible, meaningful way that allows lay readers to see a clear picture of the offender. These skills are gathered during the formal educational process.

We would generally expect a sex offender therapist to have obtained a professional degree in one of the disciplines related to social services. These degrees include Master of Social Work, Master of Counseling, doctorates in counseling and psychology, or an M.D. with a specialization in psychiatry.

As mentioned above, *formal* academic training is not available in this specific area. Thus we view academic training as less important than the other areas we will discuss. The basic degree should be in place, but the real work of deciding qualifications will hinge on the extent to which the therapist in question possesses solid clinical experience, specialized knowledge, and the requisite skills and personal qualities.

Interviewing a therapist about what was learned while in school may be time ill spent. The therapist is likely to have grasped the basics while pursuing a degree. It may be enough to know (and verify) these formal qualifications. However, what the therapist knows about treating sexual deviancy will be much more clearly shown by what the therapist does when working with sex offenders than by documentation of having graduated from an accredited institution.

Workshops and seminars attended by the therapist provide additional education. They also provide clues about expertise. Such forums are a primary means of transmitting new information about sex offender treatment issues. New research, technological innovations, and medical and pharmacological approaches are frequently presented and discussed in these settings. As knowledge regarding this field of treatment is relatively new and is expanding, a therapist who does not regularly attend workshops may not be up to date on the latest evaluation and treatment techniques. A listing of workshops, topics, presenters, and dates attended will help to evaluate the therapist's current knowledge.

Another method of acquiring current information is through reading professional journal articles, books, and so on. While not allowing for discussion, reviewing the literature a therapist has read does provide new information. A bibliography of what he or she has read will also help to determine whether or not the therapist has kept current with the latest information.

CLINICAL EXPERIENCE

Clinical experience is at the heart of a therapist's qualifications for treating sex offenders. The therapist may, as a part of the vita, provide information about prior clinical experience or internships. The typical therapist will have more than one type of experience, perhaps having worked in corrections, in a community mental health center, with a substance abuse program, or in private practice prior to treating sex offenders.

The therapist may treat a variety of complaints rather than sex offenses exclusively. This is not a problem as long as a *substantial* portion of the current practice involves treatment of sex offenders *or* the therapist has had long-term experience in treating sexual deviancy. A therapist who has never seen more than the occasional sex offender is not likely to have developed the experience or the savvy to handle their special problems.

It is our belief that superior clinical experience may substitute for an absence of academic training but that the very best of academic training cannot take the place of quality clinical experience.

Prior clinical experience should include work with involuntary clients. Sex offenders rarely come to treatment without some external motivation or pressure, often from the courts. Thus any appearance of self-motivation may be illusory. It will tend to fade over time and may disappear entirely once the potential for sanctions seems more remote. If the therapist does not have the expertise to deal with a client who approaches treatment from a defensive, manipulative, or deceptive posture, then the therapist will be unprepared for some of the most important clinical issues.

Several other factors are also important to consider. These include the length and types of treatment experience of a therapist, the clientele worked with in the past, how the therapist fit into the staff organization, and details about the actual work content and responsibilities of the therapist. A review of this information will help to evaluate the relevance of prior experience to the assessment and treatment of sexual deviancy.

There are generally three ways a therapist will have gained experience in treating sex offenders. One is by working with this population in an institution (hospital, prison, residential facility, or the like). A second method is by working in a community-based agency or nonresidential treatment facility. The third is by treating this client population in a community-based private practice.

The therapist who first treats sex offenders in an institutional setting will likely have spent a year or more under the supervision of an experienced clinician. These programs are often found within a prison setting or in a secure wing of a mental hospital. Here, sex offenders tend to be described as character disordered, sociopathic, or psychopathic, but generally they are viewed as in touch with reality.

The nature of the program itself is of interest. A therapist should be able to describe in clear terms his or her role in that program. Some programs provide self-directed therapy where minutes or tapes of sessions run by the offenders themselves are later reviewed. The review may be done by graduate students or by those who are completing a postgraduate internship. As such, the therapist may have little direct contact with offenders. Other approaches involve the therapist participating directly in the group, with interns learning alongside more experienced staff.

Other items of interest include the size of the program, the length of time individual offenders are in the program, and where offenders came from on entering treatment. The issues related to program type and size are the following:

(1) the therapist's opportunity to be directly involved with offenders,
(2) the limits the program size may have on the variety of offending patterns experienced,
(3) the range of treatment modalities a therapist is able to observe or practice, and
(4) the access the therapist might have to experienced staff for supervision and training.

A well-trained therapist should have had direct experience in assessing and treating offenders. Observations and theoretical understandings of offenders are not adequate. The therapist who has encountered a wide variety of offending behavior patterns rather than one or two variations is preferred. Access to and practice with a number of different treatment methods is superior to experience in only a few approaches. Close supervision by an experienced clinician is preferable to supervision by a generalist or one with no expertise in treating sex offenders.

The length of time offenders remained in treatment may also be significant. Some programs set release dates depending on an offender's individual progress; other programs set release dates regardless of an offender's progress. These two types of programs are likely to have quite different approaches to treatment. The first will be more likely to adopt a comprehensive set of treatment modalities, including behavioral treatment, cognitive restructuring, and social skills development components. These programs usually focus on stages of progress and clear indicators of achievement that must be completed before moving on to the next stage of therapy. Programs that receive offenders with predetermined release dates will be more likely to try an accelerated educational approach, providing as much information to offenders as possible. They may also try to set the stage for the offender to seek treatment on his own once he has been released. Therapists with experience in the first type of program generally have a broader spectrum of treatment experiences and are better prepared to treat offenders in the community.

Knowing the setting from which offenders came before entering treatment provides useful information. Where community-based treatment is a readily available alternative, only offenders who cannot adhere to outpatient community safety guidelines or who are clearly more dangerous are likely to be institutionalized. Those who are convicted in jurisdictions where community options are limited are more likely to be sent directly to an institution. Prison programs may also have populations that are viewed as tougher (or more in need of secure detention) than those in hospital programs. Finally, programs that intercept offenders on the way into prison may have a substantially different population to work with than those made up of offenders who have already been in prison for months or years.

The therapist trained in an institutional setting who later treats offenders as outpatients must learn how to replace institutional walls and monitoring with other methods designed to safeguard the community. These include establishing clear behavioral rules, communicating with other professionals and the family, developing a sense of warning signs that might signify imminent reoffense, and adjusting to new methods of controlling the offender, which may include the use of polygraph examinations to verify the offender's self-report.

A community therapist should be able to show clearly how treatment skills were acquired. Some therapists' skills are well known by virtue of their having worked at nationally known hospitals or treatment agencies. Most therapists, however, will need to demonstrate how they acquired their expertise.

Be aware that, as knowledge, experience, and resources change, both programs and therapists may alter their approach to treatment. Hopefully, this leads to improved service, although this may not always be the case. An example of change for the better might be an increase in the understanding and availability of physiological assessment tools such as the polygraph and plethysmograph. Agencies originally skeptical of these tools are increasingly integrating them into the evaluation and treatment of sex offenders.

The number of offenders evaluated and treated is also important. When a therapist states that "a majority of my clients" have been sex offenders, or that a practice was predominantly made up of offenders, it is hard to tell what this means. Actual (or estimated) numbers of clients give a much better indication of the therapist's experience. A therapist who worked in an institutional setting should indicate the number of clients for whom he or she had *primary* responsibility rather than all whose with whom he or she had contact.

It is also important to know the nature of the therapist's responsibility for the offender. Was therapy taking place, or was the contact of a monitoring nature? Was the therapist responsible for assessing initial needs, deficits, and levels of deviancy and preparing therapeutic strategy, or for seeing that a particular regimen or educational component was carried out? Generally, there is a progression of increasing responsibilities as the therapist becomes more familiar with the work.

In summary, each therapist needs to carefully outline the nature of work experience and describe how it is relevant to the assessment and treatment of sex offenders in a community-based setting. This will provide a clearer picture of the experience a therapist brings to the work. Some types of experiences are more valuable and better prepare a therapist to deal with sex offenders who are treated in the community.

SPECIALIZED KNOWLEDGE

To be effective, a therapist who decides to work with sex offenders must possess expertise in a variety of areas not normally encountered in a general clinical practice. Areas of knowledge that are essential include sexual deviancy and offender issues and the impact of sexual abuse on victims. Skills required include networking with criminal justice and social service agencies and an in-depth knowledge of community resources. Sexual deviancy and offender issues are dealt with at length in Chapters 5 and 6. Victimization issues were addressed in Chapter 2. These areas will only be touched on briefly here.

Sexual Deviancy and Offender Issues

The therapist must have an understanding of deviant arousal patterns, how they develop, and how to uncover and change them. Offenders usually have engaged in many sexual offenses prior to the most recently known offense. They also tend to engage in a variety of sexual behaviors rather than to have a single form of deviant sexual outlet. Indeed, each type of offense has different rates of commission per apprehension (Abel et al., 1983). Exposers generally have committed hundreds of acts and have similar numbers of victims before being cited or arrested. Intrafamilial sexual offenders, on the other hand, may have only a few victims who have been offended against many times each. Many offenders begin their offense careers as teenagers rather than as adults (Hindman, 1988). Predatory offenders often engage in cruising or casing behaviors to locate potential victims, whereas the in-family child molester may employ more subtle grooming techniques. This information is important for the therapist to know because it directly affects both the restrictions that may be recommended for the offender and the selection of treatment modalities. The therapist must be able to spot and counter defensive stances adopted by offenders. It may not always be possible to break through an offender's defensiveness. The therapist must be prepared to acknowledge when treatment is not going to be effective and must recommend alternatives for dealing with these offenders.

Because offenders tend to justify or entitle themselves to commit sex offenses, the therapist must understand cognitive distortion processes and must have methods to challenge and alter these thinking patterns. The therapist must deal with a host of ancillary issues, such as domination and manipulation, anger and aggressive outbursts, depression, self-defeating behaviors, and a variety of skills deficits.

Victimization Issues

The therapist must also be versed in the issues of victims. Offenders may describe their victims in a number of ways, from seductress to aggressor, from precocious child to blackmailer. The therapist will need to know the variety of ways in which victims may be vulnerable to being set up and molested. Understanding victims' physical, mental, and emotional areas of vulnerability is essential for a sex offender therapist.

A sex offender therapist must also understand the impact of sexual molestation on children. Challenging the cognitive distortions employed by offenders requires discussing the pressures on victims to comply and to keep secrets.

To be effective, a sex offender therapist must be able to describe the impact of the offenses on victims' lives. For example, offenders will sometimes blame their behavior on misbehaving children. They will describe their sexual assault as simply trying to connect with children and they will deny any sexual motivation. Offenders rarely see how grooming of victims may have negatively affected the victims' self-esteem and sense of ownership of their body. Thus the therapist needs to be able to help offenders see the implications of their acts from the victims' point of view so that they may also see the connection to children's behavior.

The therapist who treats sex offenders is often called on to play a role in reuniting a family where sexual abuse has occurred. In such instances, it is necessary for the therapist to understand and describe observable behavioral cues to those who will be supervising the offender's contacts with children. Indeed, it is important for the therapist to understand the need for such monitors as well as how to train them to do their work.

Finally, it is necessary for the therapist to be aware of how the nonoffending caretaker has responded to the disclosure of sexual abuse. This response has implications for how that person will react to and protect the victim. When the nonoffending parent supports the victim, the therapist can respond to family needs in a much different way than when the caretaker denies and rejects the victim or the victim's claims.

Criminal Justice Issues

As highlighted in Chapter 1, "Introduction," the therapist who treats sex offenders will be called on to acknowledge the concerns of and to interact with agents of the community, mainly the criminal justice system. A primary reason for the existence of a criminal justice system is to safeguard members of the community. While a therapist is necessarily concerned with the well-being of the individual offender, the needs of the community cannot be ignored. Thus the therapist must be willing to balance the need for safety of victims and the community against the needs of offenders. Where a strong potential for continued offending exists, the therapist must be willing to opt for community safety over the needs, and even the best interests, of the offender.

A sex offender therapist must have a competent working knowledge of the criminal justice system. This should include a general understanding of how the system is organized and the rules by which it operates, in terms of both who is accountable to whom and the laws that govern the policies and actions of the actors within the system.

Specific knowledge about the local criminal justice system is also necessary. For example, knowing which agencies investigate sexual crimes, as well as their general jurisdictions, is important for reporting new offenses. Similarly, knowing in general terms how the local system is likely to react to a given set of circumstances is helpful, both in preparing an offender for the legal consequences he is facing and in organizing a practice involving this type of client.

The therapist who has come from a clinical background where voluntary, self-motivated clients were served may find working with sex offenders to be a crowded type of practice. In most mental health treatment, the therapist is involved with the client and a family member or two. When treating sex offenders, the therapist acts as proxy for a host of other interested people. There are victims and family members who are either concerned for their own safety or for the eventual reintegration of the offender into a healthy family system. There are often victim counselors who are serving as advocates for their clients. Prosecutors and defense attorneys are interested in what is being learned about the offender and what is to be done with that knowledge. Eventually, the courts become involved, including judges. Probation officers want to know what progress is being made toward the offender's acquiring self-control to ensure community safety. The therapist is in the center of this whirl of actors and must keep each one informed of developments as the need arises.

Different levels of the criminal justice system will be encountered during the time the therapist treats each offender. Initially, police may be contacted to clarify or gather additional information that is free of the offender's bias. Child welfare agencies, schools, juvenile authorities, and a variety of others will also provide information.

The therapist will need to know who has which information, and how to get it. A law enforcement agency may be prohibited from giving police reports directly to a therapist. A defense attorney may be authorized to share the information on behalf of his client but may be delayed in receiving the reports by a need to obtain them through the discovery process in court. The local prosecuting attorney may be able to provide the most complete information, providing the case has gotten that far into the system.

The therapist treating sex offenders needs to be aware that any single source of information may be biased or incomplete for a variety of reasons. Therefore, the therapist should generally make it a practice to check information through collateral resources.

It is important to know who plays what roles in the criminal justice system so that the therapist may obtain the fastest response to inquiries and requests. For example, if an offender appears likely to violate probation conditions, a probation officer may be more helpful than the police. On the other hand, if the offender is about to violate a restraining order, the police may be the appropriate agency to contact.

Community Resources

The therapist needs to know about community resources as well as the criminal justice system to meet offenders' special needs. Skill and resource deficits can affect the nature and course that treatment may take. It is not sufficient merely to know what agencies exist: The therapist must also have some working knowledge of the criteria used to screen applicants and the services a client is likely to receive. This is important because, if offenders are referred to an agency and get lost in the shuffle, valuable time can be lost from treatment. Also, offenders sometimes are not honest about follow through with an agency. If they attempt to deceive the therapist about their experiences with that agency, the therapist with knowledge of the agency is less likely to be taken in. Finally, the therapist who identifies offenders' needs should know where to find resources to address them.

The variety of services available depends on the community where treatment is taking place. We will list several types of services that a therapist is likely to need for sex offenders or their families and will describe briefly what might be expected from each area. The areas highlighted include victim services, community protection agencies, other offender therapists, testing resources, substance abuse programs, employment services, housing services, and financial resources.

(1) Victim services. The therapist treating sex offenders focuses primarily on client needs. However, the therapist often must be in touch with other therapists who are treating the victims. During the initial phases of treatment, the therapist will address the harm caused by the sexual abuse. As offenders are not likely to be self-confrontive across the broad range of harmful consequences to their victims, the therapist may want to provide this confrontation using the actual incidents and their effects as

learned from consultation with victims' therapists (see Chapter 2, "A Primer on Victimology," for greater discussion). Contacts with victims' therapists are also essential in situations where families intend to reunite (see Chapter 7, "Reuniting Incest Offenders with Their Families").

It is generally good practice to know the capabilities of those who specialize in the treatment of sexual abuse victims. If the offender's family has not sought treatment for the victims, the sex offender therapist may need to make a referral. Victim and family treatment are critical to any plans to allow offenders access to victims and, at times, to other family members.

The therapist should be aware of support groups for mothers, treatment for adult survivors and child victims of sexual abuse, and the general cost of these services. Many states provide financial assistance to victims. The therapist should know the criteria and means of access to these funds. Local organizations may provide support for children who have been sexually abused. Hospitals, rape relief, and private citizens' groups all belong in a therapist's directory of services for victims.

(2) Community protection agencies. Some offenders pose a continuing threat to victims and other family members. These offenders may intimidate or actually attack victims. If a therapist ignores this possibility, victims could be harmed again. Intimidated victims may recant their stories rather than risk attack, thus letting offenders go free. The therapist has a duty to protect potential victims from harm (*Tarasoff v. Regents of University of California*, 1976, and *Peterson v. State of Washington*, 1983).

The therapist needs to know how to get protection for victims. Protective resources include police, the courts, probation and parole services, child protective services, women's shelters, and civil involuntary commitment proceedings.

(3) Other offender therapists. The therapist who treats sex offenders should be acquainted with others in the same field. At times, offenders desire a second opinion after reviewing their evaluations. A second opinion is appropriate and may also help offenders to confront their problems rather than allowing them to believe the problem is in the mind of the first therapist.

While all forms of therapy are demanding and sometimes draining, treating sex offenders is especially so. The process of frequent confrontations; being on guard for deception; challenging habitual, subtle thinking errors and distortions; and working with a largely nonempathic clientele is different from most other forms of treatment. Unlike most social service clientele, this client population is often out to "beat the system," which includes the therapist. The therapist may not assume that sex offenders approach treatment with the intent to be open and honest.

Consulting with other therapists may provide new ideas or insights and is often a useful way to find new avenues around treatment roadblocks. It can serve to verify who really has the problem, the therapist or the offender. Consultations help to allay the stress inherent with this work.

(4) Testing resources. It is important to know whether the therapist uses testing, how that testing is conducted, and how the results of the tests are used. (For detailed discussion of these, refer to Chapter 5, "The Sex Offender Evaluation Report.") A therapist generally uses physiological testing to check for deception and to measure relative states of arousal to different types of sexual stimuli. The polygraph and plethysmograph are most commonly used. Psychological tests are primarily used to measure character or personality traits, perceptions, and intelligence.

Other tests pinpoint specific problems, such as social adaptability, values and beliefs, specific knowledge areas, and the like. These tests are not as central to offending as those mentioned above, but they may help to identify other problems.

A therapist may not be prepared to conduct the full scope of testing that might be of benefit to the client. Specialists are available for assessments of some issues. Local community colleges, for example, can normally test for work aptitudes, interest, various knowledge levels, and some learning disabilities. Hospitals and clinics can perform medical, neurological, and psychiatric testing. The therapist should have a broad range of knowledge about where to turn for specialized testing services.

(5) Substance abuse programs. Therapy delays occur when offenders are too toxic to focus on treatment. The sex offender therapist must have sober, straight clients to work with in therapy. Treatment for sexual deviancy may have to be temporarily set aside until substance abuse issues can be resolved.

A therapist needs to recognize drug or alcohol problems as they appear and must also know what local agencies exist to evaluate, treat, and monitor these problems. Breathalyzer and urinalysis testing may be necessary as an adjunct to therapy to ensure the client's continued abstinence. The therapist should know about the local evaluating and referring sources for these problems and the recovery programs such as Alcoholics Anonymous and Narcotics Anonymous.

(6) Employment services. The therapist must know about potential employment services for offenders who need work. Although the therapist

may not attempt to place offenders, knowledge of the employment scene gives the therapist the ability to assess an unemployed offender's efforts to locate employment.

It is important that offenders have employment because it provides money to pay for living expenses and to meet other obligations, including payment for treatment. Idle time, coupled with the heavy legal problems an offender faces, may lead to depression. Employment is a source of self-esteem and demonstrates stability.

The therapist needs to be aware of local hiring cycles and trends, temporary and long-term employment services, and job training programs. Checking offenders' follow through on referrals provides clues about their stability and motivation.

(7) Housing services. Housing needs may become a treatment issue. Offenders often must move from their homes if they live with their victims. This provides safety for the victims and reduces the possibility of manipulation by the offenders. It also creates financial hardship on families if scarce funds must go to another landlord. The therapist may need to help assess available housing options and direct offenders to appropriate quarters.

Living arrangements may be with friends, relatives, or acquaintances without children, low-cost hotels or apartments, missions, shared rentals, and so on. The therapist needs to assess safety issues related to where offenders live. This calls for knowledge about neighborhood environments. It does not make sense to move child molesters away from children in their own homes and into relatives' homes where children live. The point is to have offenders living in places that do not provide or demand contact with potential victims. Both children and offenders benefit from this arrangement.

Family members may also need housing resources. Sometimes dealing with a sexually abusive family member and all of the attendant costs strains a family's budget beyond its limits. In such cases, the family may choose to move to relieve worries about being able to make a mortgage payment. The family may also choose to move because the home contains too many bad memories, and living there is a constant reminder of the victimization. If the family has run a business from the home, it may make more sense for the family to move and have the offender stay on to operate the business.

Women's shelters, emergency housing, and relatives with children (who thereby cannot provide suitable housing for offenders) may be available for other family members if no other resources exist for offenders. When possible, victims should not be further disrupted and traumatized by having to move from their homes. We view the alternative of families moving and offenders staying in the home as the last resort.

(8) Financial resources. Offenders, sometimes despite substantial incomes, often seem to be in dire financial straits. Money management skills, debt consolidation, and financial planning may be in order. The therapist should be aware of credit counseling through credit unions, banks, savings and loan associations, and other community agencies. It may also be important to know something about where to find financial planners, the current refinancing market, places to obtain debt or credit card consolidation loans, and courses in money management at local community colleges.

The sex offender therapist must make use of the wide array of services the community has to offer. Treating sex offenders is a team and community effort. The therapist who recognizes and makes use of this approach stands a better chance of assisting offenders to gain control over their behavior.

SKILLS AND QUALITIES

A therapist's personal qualities and skills must be considered when determining whether to approve a therapist for community-based treatment. As we stated in the Preface, one of the objectives of this work is to move the selection of sex offender therapists beyond the vague, biased, and anecdotal approach frequently used. Selection based on ability to protect the community as well as to effectively treat offenders is the goal. This does not mean that personal abilities and qualities do not enter into the decision. There are some factors that should be considered. We have broken these skill and personal quality factors down into three areas for discussion: (a) dealing directly with offenders, (b) dealing with the community, and (c) personal traits and abilities. Therapists should demonstrate abilities and qualities in all of these areas.

Dealing Directly with Offenders

The first category of skills and qualities a sex offender therapist must possess are those that pertain directly to working with sex offenders. These include assertiveness, confrontiveness, and the ability to avoid manipulation. While these skills may pertain to work with all offenders (Samenow, 1984, pp. xiv-xv), they are essential with sex offenders.

(1) Assertiveness. Few sex offenders are appropriately assertive. Most are passive or aggressive, often in the extreme. Dealing with offenders requires the ability to spot the ways offenders have misused this characteristic in service of their deviancy. Although the therapist may not be personally challenged by offenders, sometimes the therapist will have to hold ground and avoid either backing down from aggressive offenders or reaching out inappropriately to rescue passive ones. The therapist must be able to assume a directive stance to establish restrictions on behavior, gather necessary information, and set treatment objectives. Because clients are asked to adopt assertive methods of behavior and communication, the therapist needs to lead by example.

(2) Confrontiveness. Confrontation is unavoidable in the treatment of sex offenders. This does not mean yelling at offenders or belittling them. Confrontation has been frequently associated with aggressive behavior, but it is not synonymous with it.

Offenders engage in sexually deviant behaviors that are stimulating and pleasurable to them. Some are blocked from acceptable sexual outlets and choose a deviant outlet over no outlet. All are secretive about and protective of these behaviors. They resist revealing and changing these deviant behaviors. Similarly, they tend to resist exploration and discussion of the behaviors that support their deviancy.

Confrontation, whether gentle or forceful, is necessary for offenders to change. They will not spontaneously abandon well-practiced, cognitively supported, and emotionally satisfying actions simply because they have been discovered. Although offenders may announce intentions to change, their energies are more likely to be spent covering, defending, and rationalizing their behaviors. Promises of change may be more an attempt to avoid consequences than a reliable predictor of motivation for behavioral change.

The therapist must be willing and able to confront denial, minimization, rationalization, and deception. Confrontation creates discomfort for offenders and sometimes acute emotional pain. Offenders' initial responses to this emotional state are often attempts to get the therapist to abandon the topic. Offenders let the therapist know just how uncomfortable they feel. The therapist who fails to follow through with necessary confrontation does offenders and the community a disservice.

(3) Ability to avoid manipulation. Sex offenders are often skillful manipulators. This may spring in part from their desire for deviant sexuality coupled with their need to avoid detection. A therapist must be prepared for the variety of ways offenders try to influence the evaluation in their favor. Some of the more obvious ways include denial, minimiza-

tion, blaming, and lying. The therapist who works with offenders needs to be prepared for other manipulations as well. These include appearing especially virtuous or using time, financial pressures, and religion inappropriately. We will examine each of these areas to distinguish real problems from roadblocks.

One of the manipulations used effectively by sex offenders is to cultivate a reputation as *good and concerned people.* Neighbors recall how offenders pitch in to help with community projects; relatives describe the helpful, upbeat nature offenders display; and coworkers list the times offenders offer to work late or lend a hand with their overload. These people will find it difficult to believe that such nice men could be sex offenders who really did what they are accused of: molest a child. There must be some mistake, they will argue. Sex offenders are often the last people anyone would suspect.

The therapist may be fooled by this approach just as close friends and acquaintances are taken in. There is frequently no discernible motive for offenders to molest. Many offenders come from good families and have what appear to be happy homes, good jobs, respect from their peers, and all of the trappings of security. They may approach the therapist with a reasonable and cooperative demeanor and appear puzzled by why these poor children might accuse them of such a horrible crime.

The therapist must guard against offenders who may be skilled at getting others to see them in a positive light. These offenders will be able to quickly figure out what they think the therapist wants to hear. They will be able to relate seemingly empathic responses about the victims and, if they do admit to molesting, will display remorse and shame while indicating that their offense was an aberration and certainly not what they are really like. Rather than seeing such behavior as progress, the therapist should focus on offenders' actions and work (see Chapter 6, "Treatment Issues, Methods, and Measures of Effectiveness").

A therapist treating sex offenders frequently finds it necessary to deal with *time-related pressures.* These are not always engineered by the offender. Defense attorneys and prosecutors want evaluations quickly so they can begin to design their case strategies and negotiate outcomes. If the case is in the hands of the court by the time the therapist is called in, there may already be a sentencing date set, and the court will want the report to be included in the sentencing deliberations. Family members push for answers to questions about how long it will be before offenders are able to assume their previous duties for the family or when they will be able to come home or see the children again.

These forces may pressure the therapist to hurry through an evaluation. The therapist must not allow the evaluation, or treatment, to be undermined by such pressure but must take the time necessary to do a thorough evaluation, as detailed in Chapter 5. When work cannot be completed within the time lines required by others, the therapist should be able to produce tentative findings with the missing elements clearly stated. Report limitations should also be made clear.

Offenders' manipulations related to time usually have to do with the damage being done to the family by delays that keep the offender out of the home and away from the victims or by the cost associated with long-term treatment. In these cases, offenders will try to make the therapist feel guilty or responsible for the pain that the offenders or their families are experiencing in an attempt to speed up the process or to sidetrack it from unpleasant segments of therapy. This form of manipulation is a treatment issue, and the therapist must not overlook it.

Sex offenders frequently have *financial problems* in addition to their sexual deviancy. Many cannot account for the distribution of their monthly incomes and do not have any type of budget or financial plan. Even when this is not the case, the discovery of the deviancy may precipitate a personal financial crisis. Offenders will need to hire attorneys, move from the home, or, where the children have been removed, pay for foster care arrangements. Offenders also must pay for the costs associated with evaluations, testing, and treatment. Some may lose their jobs as the result of their crimes being disclosed.

As with time pressures, the therapist must be able to evaluate the legitimacy of claims of financial hardship. The reality is that offenders must reprioritize their spending patterns, but they frequently do not wish to do so. When an offender asks that treatment be suspended or shortened due to a lack of money, the therapist has to look at all of the resources available to the offender before making such a decision. Offenders may have to choose between losing their homes, automobiles, recreational properties, and retirement funds or dropping out of treatment and possibly going to prison. Because none of these choices is attractive, the therapist must be prepared for offenders to manipulate for premature completion of treatment.

Offenders' criminal behaviors have tremendous financial impact on their families. Unfortunately, the pain, suffering, and other consequences for these families do not end at the point of disclosure. They are likely to feel the ripple effects of the sexual abuse in many ways for years.

The therapist should not be manipulated by such situations into lowering treatment standards or expectations for offenders. Offenders are not well served if they are rescued from the impact or consequences of their crimes. Rather, they need to be shown how, in the midst of these difficulties, to rectify their decision-making processes and to accept responsibility for the harmful choices they have made.

It is not uncommon to encounter offenders who profess to be devoutly religious. Some of these offenders have been involved in their religion for years, whereas others have experienced a conversion following their arrest for their crimes.

A strong *religious belief* may present opportunities or pitfalls for the therapist. Sometimes offenders will contend that, having accepted their religious beliefs, they are saved and delivered from the evil that caused them to offend. As a result, these offenders will maintain that they are no longer in need of counseling. They will be protected from future temptations to offend. They may also maintain that secular authority has little jurisdiction over them as they are concerned, via their religion, with their eternal lives.

"You are talking about my life here on Earth," they may say. "I am concerned with my eternal soul, and that is more important to me than life here on Earth." Because they have professed their faith, they can claim divine forgiveness. They may appear insulted at the suggestion that they are to be held accountable for anything that happened *before* they were saved.

Offenders can misuse virtually anything in service of their sexual deviancy. Religion is no exception and may be twisted to serve deviancy in a variety of ways. Offenders may challenge a therapist by asking about the therapist's Christian beliefs and then claim that, because the therapist does not agree *completely* with their own biblical interpretations, they are unable to accept direction over their personal lives from the therapist. They may frequently quote from the Bible, interpreting passages as giving them authority for their views and actions. Offenders may bring their church leaders to treatment with them, hoping to pressure the therapist into abandoning some or all of the treatment modalities the therapist might use to make deviant sexuality less attractive. (Masturbatory conditioning is a favorite target.) A few offenders will even threaten lawsuits against the therapist if they feel their religious beliefs are being abridged.

A therapist must be able to avoid this manipulation. It is often possible to co-opt strong religious beliefs to help with the treatment process. Working with clergy is often helpful. Although offenders may have groomed their religious authorities to believe that the therapist is an agent of the devil who proposes that they engage in unholy acts or thoughts, most clergy are able to work through this misinformation campaign. Many may be uninformed about the dynamics of sexual offending, but they do understand how fear, shame, temptation, and secrecy work. The language used by clergy and therapists may differ, but the underlying concepts are very similar. Both parties are interested in the health of offenders, although one may speak of mental health while the other calls it spiritual health. Both rely on offenders' becoming honest, facing their problems, and gaining the strength to deal with them. Both believe that people can change, grow, and develop healthier attitudes and behaviors.

Religious faith may provide strength to assist offenders in examining themselves in detail, stripping away the defenses, distortions, and manipulations that allowed the offending to take place. But therapists should state clearly that treatment cannot proceed when the offender uses religion inappropriately as a barrier to the therapeutic process.

Dealing with the Community

There are three main issues relating to how a therapist works within a community. These are (a) a team treatment orientation, (b) dealing with confidentiality, and (c) a concern for community safety. How therapists handle each of these issues indicates their skill in working with sex offenders in community-based treatment.

(1) A team treatment orientation. Those who are responsible for selecting the therapist should consider the therapist's ability to work with others in a team approach. Because a goal of therapy with sex offenders is to increase their ability to control their deviant impulses and behaviors, the therapist will need feedback from others who have occasion to observe offenders outside the clinical setting. Sex offenders frequently become adept at manipulating people they encounter, and the therapist is subject to this approach as well. He or she is much more open to manipulation when working in isolation with offenders. The therapist's team should include probation officers, child welfare advocates, and ministers and counselors working with other family members. Responsible family members, employers, and friends should not be overlooked.

As a team member, the therapist should take an active role in establishing and maintaining contact with others who have a shared interest in the case. Contacts by telephone, in person, and by written reports are all important methods of sharing information about offenders in treatment. Telephone contact is a two-way medium, prompting questions and feedback on observations by both parties. Written reports record the initial issues and concerns of the therapist and may later highlight emerging problems, memorialize treatment phase completions, and record the eventual completion of treatment. Personal contacts, like telephone contacts, serve as a broader avenue of communication.

(2) Dealing with confidentiality. The manner in which a therapist handles confidentiality is an important factor to consider. The therapist who will not discuss relevant, intimate details about offenders with others who need to know should not be chosen to work with this population.

Confidentiality in psychotherapy has grown out of the presumed need to reassure patients that they may freely discuss even the most intimate and embarrassing details of their thoughts and behaviors without fear that this information will be disclosed to others. We argue that, in the community-based treatment of sex offenders, safety issues must override the usual rights to confidentiality. Sex offending against children is, by its very nature, a secretive behavior. A major goal for community-based treatment of sex offenders is to strip away the secrecy that surrounds the molesting. Offenders must take responsibility for their own thoughts, feelings, and actions. These goals are not met when a therapist gets caught up in helping offenders to maintain secrecy. In treating sex offenders, confidentiality does not protect the community.

Offenders do not tend to be fully open and honest about their sexual thoughts and behaviors, even with themselves (Dreiblatt, 1982). In fact, a therapist must often consult with collateral information sources to get a closer approximation of the truth than offenders generally offer. The police may have records indicating prior contacts or arrests for sexual offenses that offenders failed to disclose to the therapist. Police records or a current or former spouse may also disclose past instances of domestic violence that offenders omit from descriptions of their marriage. Other family members may recall that they, too, have been victims of these offenders. Victim counselors may receive more detailed accounts of the molesting than offenders divulge.

As discussed in Chapter 1, sex offenders seldom come to treatment without an outside push, such as the threat of criminal charges. Because the community is defining the existence of a problem and making the referral, community supervision agents have a legitimate expectation to be kept apprised of evaluation and treatment progress. As they may be responsible for sanctioning status changes for offenders, such as contact with former victims or offenders moving back into their homes, they must be kept informed. The therapist needs to insist on this departure from the traditional model of confidentiality. Understanding that they will be asked to share information about offenders, therapists will inform their clients in advance and obtain the necessary releases.

(3) Concern for community safety. Finally, a therapist will encounter the problem of how to protect community safety while treating sex offenders. The therapist will, among other things, have to form an opinion about which sex offenders are acceptable risks for community treatment and which are not. Some offenders are not capable of dealing with treatment and their daily life in the community while controlling their urges to offend. Although some go through a period of abstinence and lowered sexual drive related to the fear they experienced at being caught, this may only be a temporary hiatus that is not indicative of long-range ability to control sexual impulses.

The therapist must be prepared to recommend that the offender be incarcerated. This runs counter to the belief of many therapists who tend to see prison as more of a problem than a solution. It is not generally in the best interests of offenders to be sent to prison. Freedom is limited and opportunities for treatment may be remote. Also, the probability of personal harm coming to offenders who molest children may be high in a prison setting. However, those who treat sex offenders are frequently required to choose between the best interests of offenders and the best interests of the community. They may have to enforce treatment conditions requiring offenders to leave their homes, prohibiting them from seeing their children, limiting their sexual and/or social activities, requiring them to change their careers, and in other ways taking steps that severely affect their lives. Recommending incarceration is one of the hard choices the therapist must face. We are not advocating that the therapist usurp the judicial function in establishing offenders' punishment. We are recommending that the therapist must be willing and able to make a clear statement about the assessed risk a given offender presents to the community.

Personal Traits and Abilities

As discussed in the introductory chapter, treating sex offenders is especially demanding work. The therapist who does this work requires some special personal traits and abilities. Although we have attempted to point out the most necessary traits and abilities, we recognize that this single area may provide the greatest controversy. Our advice is to use these guidelines as a point of departure for discussion.

Our discussion will center on six qualities that we think are necessary for a therapist who treats sex offenders in a community setting. The therapist must possess the following attributes:

(1) the ability to cope with stress
(2) the ability to discuss sexual matters openly
(3) the ability to be precise
(4) the ability to maintain objectivity
(5) the ability to remain realistic about sex offenders
(6) freedom from a deviant/criminal history

Without these basic attributes, a therapist will have difficulty providing the level of service to clients and safety to the community that are necessary.

(1) The ability to cope with stress. Treating sex offenders produces a variety of highly stressful situations for the therapist. The therapist will encounter family members whose reactions vary from blaming victims and denying the assaults to those who want offenders punished and would like the therapist to be an instrument of retribution. Either of these groups may turn on the therapist if its position is not supported.

The therapist also encounters situations where nonoffending spouses reveal for the first time that they, too, were victims of sexual abuse but have not told anyone about it until now. Therapists will see some families disintegrate, victims who turn on themselves and engage in self-destructive behaviors, offenders who choose suicide over dealing with their crimes, and some families struggling with entirely new ways of relating to each other while trying to survive, rebuild, and reunite. As described in Chapter 2, victims may recant. In these instances, the therapist is likely to be subjected to pressure from offenders and family members, including the victim, to report to the authorities that the victim lied. At times the therapist will have to see offenders who have undoubtedly committed sexual offenses against children go free.

Sexual abuse cases provide a host of opportunities for encountering stress. Emotions of offenders and their families run the gamut from despair and fear to anger and disbelief. Their actions may range from collapse and immobility to acting out in violent ways. The therapist working with this population must be prepared to deal with this range of feelings and actions as they arise and to assess them for their impact on therapy.

A therapist who is not prepared for this stress is likely to burn out quickly. The therapist must receive support from the other professionals in the community, just as they depend on the therapist. Without support, such as other therapists or a team of community members who deal primarily with sexual abuse matters, the community may experience a high turnover in therapists or low-quality treatment resources.

(2) The ability to discuss sexual matters openly. Although it may seem too obvious to mention, a sex offender therapist must be capable of discussing sexual matters without reservation. A frank and thorough assessment of the offender's sexual thinking is essential, both during the initial evaluation and throughout the course of treatment. The therapist must manage the sequence of treatment events to tailor treatment to specific needs. This cannot happen if the therapist is hesitant about discussing sexual matters. Full disclosure is essential to breaking through denial, and it ultimately allows offenders the opportunity to see and address their full range of deviancy. Until they are able to do this, they cannot counteract their inappropriate conditioning and thinking. These tasks cannot be accomplished when a therapist is unable or unwilling to discuss all aspects of sex in an explicit manner without embarrassment or hesitation.

Not all therapists are comfortable with this aspect of the work. Sexual matters have long been taboo issues of discussion in our society. People joke and talk superficially about sex but do not normally discuss in detail sexual thoughts, fantasies, or actions. People certainly do not routinely question others about the intimate details of their sexual lives. We are generally too concerned with individual privacy and sexual taboos to do this.

However, this is at the heart of what the sex offender therapist must be concerned about to be effective. We maintain that sex offenders need to be in treatment because of their sexual behavior, not because of other family issues. The therapist who cannot or will not deal with sexual issues without reservation should not be treating sex offenders.

A therapist must do more than accept the official version of the offense as presented in the police reports or in the victim's statement. Offenders usually do not tell the complete truth about the offending, especially to the police. They certainly do not volunteer information about other deviant sexual practices that would make them look more deviant than is already known. Victims, too, sometimes minimize the extent of the sexual activity when they disclose. The therapist must be prepared to probe and question, review disclosures with the victim's counselor, and verify what is learned by use of the polygraph.

Initial disclosures by sex offenders are normally only the beginning of the whole truth about their sexual deviancy. An exhaustive review of sexual history and current sexual behavior is essential. The therapist needs to be concerned about the existence of other undiscovered victims. The extent of deviancy must be known if an effective treatment plan is to be devised. Offenders' early sexual experiences, development of deviant and other sexual arousal patterns, and conditioning through masturbation must all be explored.

Even offenders' definitions of sexual behavior must be scrutinized. Defining sexual behavior in nonsexual terms is a common form of minimization. Offenders who masturbate frequently may define their behavior as relieving tension. When asked about their sexual thoughts, they may deny having any. In their minds, masturbation and the thoughts that accompany it do not count because, by their definition, they are engaged in relieving tension rather than engaging in sexual behavior. Offenders thus frequently fail to recognize sexual thoughts. If a therapist is not explicit, probing, and willing to confront the offender about exactly what goes on in the offender's mind, the core of sexual deviancy may be left intact.

(3) The ability to be precise. Another characteristic desirable in a sex offender therapist is precision. If a therapist is going to work with offenders who have the potential to reoffend, it is necessary that the therapist pay attention to details that might serve to prevent such behavior. Attention to detail embodies accuracy, objectivity, and a clear enjoyment of the investigative aspects of this work.

Accuracy is central to the work the therapist undertakes. Overstating the case against offenders may cause undue fears, whereas minimizing may represent tacit acceptance or approval of offending and lead to unsafe decisions regarding the offender's remaining at large in the community.

Offender therapists must possess an interest in the investigative nature of their work. There is a need for continual probing for contrary evidence. Information needs to be gathered, sorted, verified, and placed in context. Rather than trusting the client as the sole, or even the best, source of information about himself, the therapist must seek independent views from those who know the offender. The therapist needs to be intrigued, rather than put off, by the process of gathering all the data and seeking the lie or inconsistency.

(4) The ability to maintain objectivity. Treating sex offenders is a long and difficult process. Problems that have taken years to develop are not set aside is a few sessions, even with the most qualified and experienced therapist and the most willing clients. When considering a particular therapist as a resource for sex offenders, it is necessary to keep in mind that the attitude of the therapist is nearly as important as the attitude of the offender. A therapist may be overly optimistic about his or her own ability or the offender's ability to change behavior. If the therapist cannot understand sexual attraction to children, he or she may underestimate the

attraction for offenders. Thus the therapist may take a superficial approach to treatment.

On the other hand, burnout and cynicism from working with sex offenders are also possible. A therapist who has seen too little success may become jaded and disinterested in providing full treatment.

Objectivity and personal balance are key elements. The therapist must frequently sort through conflicting versions of events. Even though the details of offenses are frequently gruesome or repellent, the therapist must avoid being swayed by personal feelings in order to clearly evaluate the offender. This is not to say that deviant behaviors are ignored, but that the therapist must be able to set aside personal feelings and dispassionately report the findings. *The job of deciding guilt or innocence and assessing sanctions is not the role of the therapist.*

The therapist treating sex offenders must maintain a balance between the knowledge that sex offenders do not readily give up their sexual deviancies and the belief that they can change given sufficient motivation, information, conditioning, and alternatives.

(5) The ability to remain realistic about sex offenders. To be successful, therapy of any type generally requires that clients perceive a problem, retain the willingness to work on the problem until it is resolved, and possess the abilities and resources needed to follow through with treatment. Not all clients are capable of or willing to change. This is especially true for sex offenders.

For sex offenders, stripping away distortions and rationalizations means facing guilt and shame and admitting to one of our society's most condemned behaviors. Denial is often preferable for many offenders. Many who are offered the opportunity to change their offending behavior will take advantage of treatment as a method of avoiding more stringent consequences.

Some offenders will continue to offend even while in therapy. A sex offender therapist *must* remain alert to this possibility. The reality is that eventually this will happen, even in the best of therapy programs. Change cannot be guaranteed, so the best that a therapist can do is to remain watchful for preoffense warning signs and contact the appropriate authorities when an offense appears imminent.

The community needs to be sure that the therapist has the experience to recognize when therapy is being used inappropriately and the willingness to call a halt to treatment when this happens. In cases where the offender is not making progress, the community should be asked to explore other alternatives for the offender that provide for community safety.

A therapist treating sex offenders must be skilled in a number of areas that are not common to other types of counseling. He or she must be able to hold ground assertively when offenders challenge the therapist's values or actively attempt deception. The therapist must constantly confront offenders' distorted thinking, attempts to avoid dealing with their sexual deviancy, and inappropriate attitudes and behaviors.

The sex offender therapist must coordinate with clients and a variety of other professionals. He or she must be personally prepared and able to deal with the pressures presented when treating sex offenders. The therapist must gather large amounts of information from a variety of sources quickly and accurately synthesize these facts into clearly stated assumptions and recommendations. Community-safety issues must be a constant, primary consideration. Amid all the competing pressures from victims, families, offenders, and the community, the therapist must maintain objectivity and clear thinking. Finally, the therapist who undertakes treatment of this population must be realistic about what motivates sex offenders to commit their crimes and the likelihood that they will be unwilling to give up their sexual deviancy.

(6) Freedom from a deviant/criminal history. Sex offender therapists, perhaps more than any other single group of mental health professionals, bear a clear and far-reaching responsibility to the community in which they practice. Even though it is seldom clearly stated, the authority and responsibility for community safety from sex offenders is delegated to the therapist to a large degree. (Community supervision agents maintain this authority and responsibility de jure, but they are easily rendered ineffective by the therapist in cases where the therapist fails to inform them of treatment violations or general lack of progress by the offender.) Because community safety depends so heavily on the therapist, it is in the community's interest that the therapist have "a healthy value system and a personal background devoid of pathology" (Jensen & Jewell, 1988, p. 14).

The idea of addicts helping addicts has been used successfully in several areas. Alcoholism and drug treatment are two examples. There is some appeal to the idea of sex offenders being helped by former offenders. However, our experience suggests a *very* cautious approach here. As discussed in Chapter 1, sex offenders are different. Compared with people who have battled other forms of compulsive behavior, sex offenders have particular trouble with personal boundaries, cognitive distortions, and realistic assessment of reoffense risk. These are areas that are critical to successful evaluation and treatment of sexual deviancy. Moreover, these problem areas do not tend to be transitory or situational but are a basic part of the sex offender's personality and behavioral structure (Nichols &

Molinder, 1984). That is precisely why sexual deviancy should never be considered "cured," but only in remission and under control.

An additional concern is that, to be effective, the offender therapist must work with the victims of sexual offenders at some level. When there is a victim therapist involved in the case, the offender therapist normally coordinates with this professional for mutual assistance in dealing with the clients. Frequently conjoint therapy meetings are held where this is useful for the victim. In cases where the victim is refusing treatment but wants to be reunited with the offender, the initial work of assessing the appropriateness of contact falls to the offender therapist. If the therapist is a former offender, the result in these cases means putting a victim under some control by a former offender.

Although there may be a place for former offenders in the recovery process of practicing offenders, it is not as sole or primary therapist. A community must consider the relative consequences in taking the risk posed by allowing recovering sexual offenders to treat practicing offenders.

A final word of caution is in order. A community will have difficulty protecting itself from those who, possessing the necessary educational credentials, will for personal gain cynically or corruptly abuse a community's trust. Nearly any credentialed therapist who has read this work would be able to make a convincing case for having the ability to treat sex offenders. It is important to periodically reevaluate their work. Those who act dishonestly, who fail to report violations, or who refuse to cooperate with community supervision agents should not treat sex offenders.

Chapter Five

The Sex Offender Evaluation Report

The first step in the process of reviewing a therapist's suitability to treat sex offenders is a review of his or her credentials. The next step is a review of the therapist's evaluation report on the offender.

While there are many uses to which the report can be put, we view it as having two basic objectives. The first is to clearly assess the offender's amenability to specialized treatment. The second is to answer the question of whether the offender can be treated in a manner that provides for community safety.

This chapter outlines the many areas that a good evaluation and report will cover. Key elements will be identified in topic headings and examples will illustrate the kinds of information that the reports should contain. We will also explain or illustrate by examples why each area is essential to a good report.

BASIC PRINCIPLES

We would stress that all reports should be characterized by thoroughness and objectivity. Thoroughness simply means covering each topic area at a depth that is appropriate to its importance. It also means gathering and checking information from many different sources. An offender's sexual history should always be covered as completely as possible because it bears so heavily on the offense itself and the issue of whether the offender can be treated successfully and safely in the community. Brevity would be appropriate in areas bearing little relevance to the current offense or to the offender's current circumstances. For example, an offender's military history might be relatively insignificant for a 72-year-old offender but highly significant for an offender who is 25 years old.

Objectivity primarily means the report specifies the data relevant to the offender and to the therapist's final conclusions. The report will also specify the sources used to gather the data. As well as the thoroughness, the quantity and quality of the data will set the tone for the report. Including the relevant, essential information allows the reader to make an independent judgment about the offender in question. Also, with data included, the reader is able to check the validity of the information independently. When significant information is omitted, the reader is unable to raise appropriate questions about the offender and his risk to the community.

High standards for thoroughness and objectivity make sex offender evaluations and reports unique in the social service field. At first glance, the reader might wonder whether such expectations are realistic. However, given the risk represented by sex offenders, the extra effort on the therapist's part is warranted. Through experience, therapists will develop routines and the organizational ability to pull together the large amounts of information we outline here. Such high standards for thoroughness and objectivity are already expected and routinely being met in some localities.

We recognize that communities differ in their abilities to provide such a rigorous approach to evaluating and treating sex offenders. Some communities lack therapists with the knowledge and expertise to apply all that we are about to describe. If we appear to have unusually high expectations, it is our intention to point the direction in which we believe evaluation and treatment of sexual offenders should go. We hope the reader will not be dissuaded because the end seems unattainable but will recognize instead that the degree of rigor, thoroughness, and caution that we suggest is attainable through a cooperative effort by those people involved in the selection of therapists and those people responsible for the treatment of sex offenders.

The reader should expect certain other characteristics in a good evaluation and report process. The therapist should avoid becoming unduly influenced by an offender's personality. Offenders tend to view the therapist as having the power to persuade the courts to allow them to stay free while in treatment. They often make every effort to please and impress the therapist. As a result, the therapist should gather data from many different sources in addition to the offender's self-report. The therapist should also clearly distinguish between the data and the interpretation of the data so that opinions and conclusions do not become treated as facts. The report should emphasize the offender's actual behaviors, especially behaviors that are relevant to risk. Finally, the report should not omit or slant data to support the therapist's conclusion but provide all relevant data. Only by this means can parties come to their own conclusions about the risk the offender presents to the community.

Certain areas should always receive prominent attention in both the evaluation process and the evaluation report. The offender's criminal offense and other criminal history should always be discussed thoroughly, and other sexually deviant patterns should be explored and reported as well. The offender's truthfulness and cooperation should be described, and the basis on which the evaluator assessed his truthfulness should be made explicit.

Our experience makes it clear that the evaluation must precede therapy. This allows for establishing benchmarks by which future changes and progress in treatment can be measured. More important, this procedure allows for assessment of risk. The imposition of sufficient structure to prevent reoffense is the first order of business. This is in keeping with our assumption that community safety and the prevention of further victimization are the primary goals of any attempt at treatment.

By setting out clear and strong conditions of therapy, the evaluation provides for the community's safety. It also makes clear to the offender that sex offender treatment is different from other forms of therapy. By concentrating on the identification of specific behavior patterns, for example, sex offender evaluation and therapy are often very focused and therapist directed. Unlike most other therapies, the evaluation process can be a reminder to the offender that the therapist has special responsibilities with respect to the community.

At times, the evaluation process may result in tentative recommendations, diagnoses, or treatment plans. There are legitimate reasons for tentative recommendations and for incomplete evaluation reports. They may result from essential material being unavailable for reasons beyond the therapist's control, or legal matters may compel completion of a report in a time frame that does not allow as thorough an evaluation as is desirable. However, such occurrences should be considered the exception, not the rule. The reasons for an incomplete assessment should be stated clearly in the report.

For a variety of reasons, the reader should be skeptical of reports that lack any significant data. First (as will be discussed in greater depth below), offenders are often expert at concealing significant information about themselves. Second, they may try to use the time limitations of the legal process to their advantage; for example, offenders may create smoke screens (consciously or unconsciously) to delay and disrupt the evaluation process, such as providing interesting but irrelevant information to keep the therapist from focusing on other, more important areas. This wastes the limited time allowed before the report must be submitted to the court. Offenders use this tactic to avoid talking about significant sexual thoughts, urges, and experiences and other issues related to their cases. Finally, information that is lacking in reports may be the kind that would have a significant bearing on the court's disposition.

Significant gaps in information may be an indication of other serious problems, for example, the therapist may not understand the need for the information or its relevance to evaluation and treatment. Gaps in information may suggest that the therapist is uncomfortable dealing with a particular area of inquiry. Another possibility is that the therapist may not feel competent to deal with certain areas or subject matter. Finally, the reader should consider whether significant therapeutic errors may be occurring, for example, simply forgetting to ask about something important. The reader should be concerned that, when significant gaps occur in reports, there is less assurance that the therapist is dealing with the issues thoroughly.

The material we are presenting here should help the reader evaluate the therapist's report. Our ideas are presented as a flexible guide. Each topic we discuss may or may not apply to any individual case, and the reader must judge whether a specific item is essential to a report. We can supply guidelines to assist the reader in this task, but the reader must apply the judgment for the process to work.

If a report lacks an element that appears important, then certain questions should be raised. Why is the element lacking? Is it important? Is its absence explained? Could the information have a significant bearing on the report if it were known? The following discussions should help readers make better judgments regarding evaluation reports. If a reader is not satisfied with a report, our material will help identify specific areas that are not satisfactory. This approach lends itself to a more objective, open, and conscious discussion of the report, the therapist, and the offender.

We have chosen to divide the discussion of evaluation reports on sex offenders into six separate content areas: (a) the offense behavior, (b) personal history and social functioning, (c) sexual history, (d) test results, (e) conclusions and recommendations, and (f) treatment conditions. Although this division makes sense to us, there is no compelling reason for a therapist to follow this format. It is not our intention to provide a rigid framework that all therapists must follow. Rather, we are outlining content areas that a good evaluation report will include. Certainly, an orderly presentation facilitates understanding. Professionally organized material may well reflect care and competence in therapy. The six categories will assist you in understanding our material. We hope they will also encourage therapists to organize their material in a fashion that is readily accessible and understandable to the readers.

THE OFFENSE BEHAVIOR

Defining the offense behavior is the initial task for the therapist when evaluating a sex offender. By offense behavior we refer to the physical acts that occurred during the offense as well as a variety of other elements. Understanding an offense requires more than a simple recounting of the crime. An explanation of how the offense was conceived and carried out is as important as describing who was directly or indirectly involved in the offense. Many nonsexual behaviors, which will be discussed below, are significant in both evaluating and treating the sex offender. Finally, the offender's point of view is critical. Comparing the offender's perspective with all the other information gathered will highlight important discrepancies. Clarifying these discrepancies is a keystone to understanding the offender and assessing his amenability to treatment, and it will also be a clear indicator of how the therapist approaches treatment.

The discussion of offense behavior is divided into the following sections: (a) antecedent behaviors, (b) victim elements, (c) significant others, (d) elements of the offense, (e) other deviant behaviors, and (f) the offender's perspective.

Antecedent Behaviors

A thorough sexual deviancy evaluation looks at more than the mere facts of the event. It also covers the offender's behaviors leading up to the offense. In only the rarest of cases is a sexual offense a single event occurring spontaneously without at least some minimal preparation that enabled the offense to occur. Understanding these precursors to offending allows better decisions and recommendations for both community safety and treatment.

The therapist must be sensitive to the amount of preparation that an offender made, taking care to consider whether the offender's account corresponds to the other information known. Did the offender take a great deal of risk in committing the offense, or did he minimize the chances of getting caught? Taking a great risk may well describe a person who is so compulsive in his sexual deviancy that he is a great risk to the community. An offender who was very cautious, on the other hand, may be one who is equally dangerous by virtue of his calculating approach. Preoffense behaviors serve as indicators a therapist must use to assess where an offender should be placed on the dangerousness continuum.

An offender can *manage risk* in a variety of ways. For example, he may minimize risk by selecting victims who are unable, or at least less likely, to reveal the offense. He may find children who were previously victimized and unlikely to respond the same way (self-protectively, for example) as a person who is being victimized for the first time, or he may choose victims over whom he exercises authority or control. Other ways that an offender may manage risk will be discussed below.

Gaining proximity to victims is another antecedent behavior of interest. A sex offender may cruise areas near schools, playgrounds, and parks and the routes nearby. He may choose residences near school grounds, parks, and other places that children frequent. He may befriend women with children who are in his target age range or younger. He may also select occupations or work schedules that bring him closer to potential victims or work schedules that increase his chances to offend.

One offender admitted during therapy that every girlfriend he had ever had during adulthood had children the ages of his sexual preference. He indicated that he had previously been unaware of how his choice of girlfriends had been guided by his sexual preference. He had not offended against all of the children, but he recognized that he continued relationships with those women who would allow him to be alone with their children and quickly discontinued relationships with those who had open and direct communication with their children about child molesters.

Interpersonal manipulation is another example of antecedent behaviors. The sex offender may befriend those who lack a strong sense of direction and are easily manipulated, those who will be dependent on him, or who are vulnerable. In this way, the offender does not have to work very hard to get what he wants. He has greater freedom from restrictions, enhancing his ability to avoid detection while offending against the chosen victim.

Antecedent behaviors may involve the use of *material resources*. The type of material used is only limited by the imagination of the offender. Experience shows that practically anything can be bent to the service of sexual deviancy. Vehicles, drugs and alcohol, money, pornography, clothing, and a variety of other items may play a part in an offender's deviant patterns.

Material resources are used in two basic ways: to aid the offender in preparing to commit his crime and to set up a victim to be assaulted. One offender may use his vehicle to cruise, searching for likely victims or locations, whereas another may use the vehicle as an enticement, trading driving lessons for sexual favors. Alcohol or other mood-altering substances may be consumed to reduce inhibitions or to establish a defense ("I was too drunk; I didn't know what I was doing"). They may also be used as a trap for victims, either to lure them into situations where offending can occur or to provide leverage to keep the victims silent ("If your mother knew you were smoking pot, she'd kill you. If you tell her about what we did I will tell her you started it when you were on drugs.").

Grooming may be the most important of all antecedent behaviors to understand. Grooming is broadly defined as any activity that desensitizes the victim or significant others for the purpose of enabling a sexual offense to occur. Victims, the family, neighbors, acquaintances, and the community may all be groomed.

There are many types of grooming, which include physical, psychological, and environmental grooming. *Physical grooming* begins with behavior that children and adults would consider appropriate. This physical contact becomes grooming behavior when it is used to accustom a victim to touching that can lead to sexual involvement. For example, the offender may use back rubs to desensitize the victim to more and more intrusive physical contact. A child sitting on an adult's lap is being groomed when the adult keeps the child there despite having an erection. Initially, the adult makes no comment or movement. If the child seems not to notice, the adult may joke about the erection. If a child shows curiosity, the adult may offer to show the child his penis. This may lead to the adult asking to see the child's genitals or to allowing the adult to touch the child. All of this is presented as a normal, nonthreatening activity.

Grooming falls in a spectrum from subtle to obvious to overt. By gaining the victim's acceptance through normal physical contact, the offender begins to break down the victim's resistance. The offender induces confusion in the victim when behavior that seemed appropriate at first becomes less appropriate. Grooming activities provide a reach-and-retreat behavioral repertoire during which the offender can test a victim's level of resistance, resolve, and vulnerability. The reach-and-retreat approach also provides a ready escape or excuse from accusations if confronted by either the child or others.

Psychological grooming many occur in a variety of ways, including the promise of material items or of special privileges. Skillful manipulation can create an indebtedness, which the offender can later use. For example, he may allow a child to stay up past regular bedtime and promise not to tell the child's mother. This works especially well when the child knows this is against the mother's wishes. It becomes even more effective when the offender is able to convince the child that, if the secret is revealed, the child will be punished rather than the offender who gave permission. Manipulations of this kind create compacts between the offender and the victim and barriers between the child and the non-offending caretaker. When offending finally begins, the child fears revealing the problem because it will lead to disclosing all of the child's other bad behaviors.

An offender may also create states of fear and uncertainty in the victim's mind. For example, the offender might read a newspaper article about another sex offender and say, "That poor man was treated unfairly, and now a cruel judge is sending him to prison for the rest of his life, just for playing with children." The offender can later use this information to manipulate the victim into agreeing not to disclose the offense. Offenders can issue covert threats with statements such as (a) "Children who do not obey their parents should be beaten," (b) "Adults know better than children what's right," or (c) "Children should not ask questions, but only do as they are told."

Some victims are especially vulnerable by virtue of their isolation, prior abuse, or other factors. The offender may present a grooming style that is immediately rewarding and pleasing to these children. He may spend special time playing, traveling, providing entertainment, or just listening and talking with a child who feels neglected. The offender may listen to the child's problems and give advice. Then, gradually, the offender may introduce his own problems, giving the child a sense of importance and wisdom by eliciting the child's advice. Grooming escalates when the offender begins to talk about problems between himself and the child's mother. He subtly or directly introduces the idea that the child can give comfort, emotional support, and love to the offender that the mother cannot or will not give because she has her own problems. The offender lays the groundwork for this kind of bond to lead to sexual exploitation later on. The effect is to create a sense that the offender and the child really understand one another. Flattery heightens the child's interest at this stage. Dwelling on the mother's problems increases the likelihood that grooming will proceed with the potential resistance of the child decreased.

Psychological grooming can make the trauma to the victim severe. The child may believe the deceits laid out by the offender, and that belief is reinforced by the memory of shared warmth and tenderness. The child's sense of importance and maturity is increased. All of these, as well as the child's sense of self-esteem and adequacy, are undermined upon disclosing the offense. Guilt, self-doubt, pain, anger, and despair are natural consequences to a child-victim of such carefully plotted grooming behavior.

An offender may also *groom other persons* to increase his access to potential victims. He may offer to do special tasks, projects, or activities for a child's mother that create the opportunity for her to be away from the home and the victim. By working long hours himself, the offender may claim that the mother should do more financially and point out the swing-shift waitress job in a city miles away. The mother may also be groomed in a negative sense by the offender constantly criticizing her, creating a desire in her to simply get away from the home. This emotional climate makes the prospects of a swing-shift or graveyard job more inviting to the mother. Without realizing it, she has been steered in a direction away from the home. The offender is now in a better position to sexually abuse the child.

Finally, *environmental grooming* occurs when the offender grooms persons outside the victim's home to increase his access to children. For example, an offender may work with children through schools or community youth groups and perform many worthwhile services. But he may also take advantage of this position and use it to arrange times to be alone with potential victims. By establishing an image of a benefactor to the community, he engenders a special trust. As a result, the mere suggestion by anyone that this person may have abused a child is often met with disbelief. The community may be inclined to side with the offender, proclaiming the impossibility of the charges because of the certainty that the offender "is just a caring individual who loves children." Once official charges have been made, those who have regular contact with and sometimes rely on the accused in various ways must then begin to grapple with what his loss will mean if he is convicted. The community may lose his committee work and his organizational or other valuable abilities. The offender often has spent much time being visible in activities that lessened the work load of those around him. This reinforces the willingness of others to put children under his care and makes the community disinclined to believe that he could do anything wrong.

In one case, a schoolteacher was convicted of sexually abusing two female students. During the presentence investigation, the probation officer received no less than 50 separate letters from supporters of the teacher. Every letter contained examples of contributions the teacher had made to the school. Other teachers described how he had made their jobs easier because of his willingness to handle less desirable extracurricular tasks. The majority of the letters referred to the victims as having bad reputations and claimed that they were at least partially to blame. Only 2 of the 50 letters showed any understanding of the basic facts of the case, which clearly indicated that the teacher had used force in his offenses. This teacher had made extensive efforts to groom an entire educational community, including students, parents, staff, and administrators.

A candid exploration and discussion of grooming behaviors by the evaluator is essential in cutting through the facade that sex offenders often construct. This facade, as long as it is permitted to stand, prevents the criminal justice system from dealing with this offender in the same objective manner in which it treats other less skillful and manipulative offenders. Allowing the facade to remain also undermines the belief in the need for effective community surveillance and supervision. Disclosure of the grooming behavior helps to penetrate the facade and to establish the appropriate structure necessary to help prevent reoffense.

A clear discussion of grooming also helps victims and other family members see how skillfully they were manipulated and how carefully structured the offender's efforts were to break down their will and sense of self-protection. This process can be instrumental in helping victims and family members break through their confusion and deal more constructively with their feelings about the offense.

Failing to break down this facade would be counterproductive to the offender and his therapy. It would allow the offender to persist in his belief that he has a host of redeeming characteristics, which are, in reality, simply a solid base for his own deviancy. The therapist who allows these virtues to persist unchallenged is not likely to recognize or challenge the true extent of the offender's deviant system. By maintaining the false image, the offender is likely to forget the psychological trauma inflicted on the victim and the toll his behavior has taken on the community as a whole. If the facade persists, the offender will not be able to examine the darker, manipulative aspects of his good deeds to see how they served as a safe base from which to initiate molesting behaviors. Understanding offender manipulation in all its forms helps explain the extent of an offender's deviancy. It also provides a basis for supervision and surveillance of an offender who is allowed to remain in the community. A thorough evaluation should consider and provide assistance to those persons responsible for community supervision by carefully analyzing these antecedent behaviors.

Victim Elements

A complete evaluation of a sex offender will include some discussion of the victim. This discussion is important for several reasons: It can help the court to carefully plan for the community's safety, for example, by illustrating how the sex offender chose his particular victim(s), and it can illustrate the depth of the offender's pathology. The discussion of the victim is one of the clearest reminders of the harm done to the victim and emphasizes the need for treatment to address the sex offender's pathology. It allows the reader to judge the importance the therapist places on victim issues. Finally, the victim may be helped by knowing that the sex offender's therapist is concerned about the harm to her.

The reader should expect to see the following issues addressed in the report. First, the report should include the *effects of the abuse*, including a description of the victim's reaction to the abuse as it was occurring. Second, the report should clarify any *special vulnerabilities* the victim may have, and how the offender took advantage of them. Next, the report should specify the *offender's attitude toward the victim*, especially any inclination to dissipate his own responsibility or the harm he has inflicted. Finally, the discussion of the victim should include a professional assessment (whenever available) of the current and *long-term impact* of the abuse.

A clear statement about the harm caused to the victim is a constant reminder to the reader of the damage caused by the offender. Frequent contacts with the offender over time tend to diminish awareness of this. Rightly or not, it is human nature that, the more time an individual spends with an offender, the more accepting of the offender as a person the individual may become. By containing a reminder of the harm caused to the victim, the evaluation demonstrates the therapist's awareness that the report plays an important role in dealing with an offender after sentencing. The report is one of the primary documents that judges, prosecutors, and probation officers may review if the offender's case comes back to court for some reconsideration, such as a probation review or revocation.

The therapist should take care to reflect the victimization in accurate terms, and neither minimize nor overstate information regarding the victim. It is essential to specify the source of any data about the victim. The therapist must bear in mind the special feelings a person may have when reporting information about the victim. For example, whereas the mother of one victim may feel deeply betrayed and angered at an offender, another mother may still want to reunite with the offender and, therefore, will minimize or even consciously distort the impact of the offense. There are many different responses that individuals may have to any one offense. For that reason, informed professional opinions may be of more value than the opinions of laypersons. Professionals who deal regularly with victims of abuse can compare one case with a number of others and are more aware of the issues pertinent to the offense. Therefore, they can be more objective in their assessment.

The evaluator can play a therapeutic role for the victim by including information about the victim's wishes in the report. This very sensitive issue can be handled in different ways depending on the factors involved in each case. It can be helpful for the victim to know that the system, including the offender's evaluator and therapist, is aware of and dealing effectively with the full nature and extent of the offense and the effect that it had on the victim.

Basic identification of a victim should be stated clearly. The report should specify the victim's age, sex, family position, and relation to the offender, as well as other appropriate data. For example, it is important to know whether the victim was especially vulnerable due to age, mental disability, or social isolation. Some victims are doubly vulnerable by virtue of their separation from or their loss of a parent. A child may have run away from a physically abusive parent only to be preyed upon by a sex offender. The life circumstances of the victim will help to more fully explain the impact of a sexual offense. An offender may use the problems of children to justify his offense, by taking advantage of these problems to commit his offense and then using them to justify his criminal behavior.

We are not persuaded by offenders who argue that children provoked their crimes. Our assumption is that adults should be held fully account-able for their own behavior. Discussions of provocative children simply mask the ways that offenders take advantage of their victims, particularly those with special vulnerabilities. One offender pointed out that his 11-year-old victim had alcohol problems, acted out sexually with a variety of men in the community, and had solicited him openly. "Besides," he said, "the girl looked like she was nearly 14 years old." Other information corroborated that the girl came from a broken home and had an alcoholic mother whose boyfriends had both physically and sexually abused her since she was quite young.

The therapist should describe additional problems that may have resulted from the crime, such as social isolation or difficulty adjusting to school. Has the victim shown new difficulties in sexual adjustment? Perhaps the victim refuses to participate in needed counseling due to the traumatic effects of the offense. Does the victim demonstrate a variety of characteristics that interfere with daily living and personal happiness, such as an inability to form friendships, fear at bedtime, or recurring nightmares? Does the victim show fear of classmates discovering the offense? Although the offender remains the focal point of the report, relevant discussion of the victim indicates a thorough evaluation.

Significant Others

Describing the other significant people in the offender's life can be important for a variety of reasons. In the discussion of antecedent behaviors above, we pointed out the possibility that sex offenders may surround themselves with people they can control and manipulate. The therapist needs to consider this likelihood during development of treatment and supervision strategies in order to limit the offender's ability to take advantage of others. Some relationships may encourage the productive use of therapy, whereas others may reinforce negative behaviors. The therapist may select information from those relatives and friends who play an important part in the offender's life. The therapist should observe how those relationships may affect the course of therapy.

The following examples illustrate the roles that significant others can play in an offender's life. If alcohol played a role in the offending behavior, friends and relatives who drink may encourage the offender to return to alcohol use. Friends or relatives of the offender are sometimes of the opinion that too much is being made of the incident and that intervention is interfering with the return to normal family life. Such attitudes may erode an offender's motivation to cooperate with treatment. An employer who does not know of the offender's crime may allow the offender to return to dangerous patterns of behavior.

In one case, an offender molested a stepson in his home, which he shared with unemployed friends. He provided them with free rent and alcohol. While they were in the home drinking with him, he molested the stepson in an adjoining room. During the investigation process, these friends minimized the offender's behavior and denied that he had any problems, especially stating their belief that he should be allowed to continue consuming alcohol. This offender had surrounded himself with friends who were willing to tolerate sexual transgressions that would shock and repel most people.

Ministers or religious counselors have a variety of attitudes about offending, forgiveness, and treatment. Partners in new romantic relationships may need to be assessed for their potential to be victimized or to foster inappropriate sexual behaviors. Others will have to be alerted to potential offense situations. Victims themselves may be inclined to seek out the offender for a variety of reasons.

It should be clear from reading the evaluation report that the therapist has paid close attention to the attitudes of the offender's significant others. Some may not be aware that the offense(s) occurred, whereas others may be informed but minimize or dispute the allegations. In each case, the therapist must evaluate the potential positive or negative influences of significant others. This sets the stage for appropriate treatment intervention while enabling judges, prosecutors, and probation officers to impose appropriate sanctions and restrictions on the offender.

Elements of the Offense

The discussion of antecedent behaviors above paves the way to a description of the offending behavior itself. Physical, psychological, and environmental aspects of the offense may be identified in the evaluation report, depending on the circumstances of each case.

A thorough, candid, anatomical accounting of the offense is imperative. This must include the people who were involved, an anatomical description of the offense, the degree of force or coercion used, and how the offender overcame the victim's resistance.

All other significant aspects of the physical assault should be included as well, especially those pertaining to the amount of force used. Force, coercion, and seduction fall along a continuum and should be discussed as such. One end of the continuum might include persuasive tactics, such as offering gifts, privileges, and promises to elicit the victim's participation in sexual activity. A greater degree of force would involve the use of threats or coercion. For example, threats of punishment or revelation of misdeeds by the child might be used to persuade the child not to resist. Physical force falls on the other end of the spectrum. Such force can include a wide range of behaviors, from arm twisting and physical restraint to punching, hitting, and even more brutal assaults. Included in this area is the use of weapons, which can range from household objects such as belts, ropes, and kitchen implements to knives and firearms. The degree of any physical restraint should be clarified. It is one thing to hold a child down with hands and body during molestation and quite another to restrain the child with ropes.

Psychological coercion, another way in which offenders induce cooperation, may be every bit as damaging as some forms of physical force. An offender who threatens to kill a child's pets, for example, may be creating a far greater long-term psychological trauma than the offender who threatens to beat a victim with, or actually uses, a belt. The evaluator should endeavor to place the degree of force used within the context of the offender's overall behavior and the victim's traumatization. This information may not be easily available to the therapist; however, when the therapist has obtained this sort of information from the victim's therapist, the value of the report is greatly increased.

The location of the offense is a natural feature of the description, whether it was the victim's or the offender's home, a car, a store, a park, the woods, a school, or elsewhere. These data and information, such as time of offense, can be instrumental in developing an effective plan of surveillance and prevention. The acts that occurred should be described in sufficient detail so that there is no doubt about what took place. If there is doubt, the ambiguity should be discussed explicitly, for example, whether fondling took place over or under a child's clothing, whether the child was undressed by the offender or undressed him- or herself, whether the child was made to touch the offender's body or his genitals, whether the offender penetrated the victim (vagina, anus, mouth), and what was used to effect the penetration (finger, tongue, penis, or objects).

The environmental aspects of the offense should be clarified when relevant. For example, if an offender molested a child while there were other adults in the immediate vicinity, this could mean that the offender was willing to take great risks or perhaps that the other adults could not be counted on to protect the potential victim in the future. This kind of information has a direct bearing on the nature of restrictions that should be placed on the offender if he is allowed to remain in the community.

A failure by the evaluator to discuss candidly and in complete detail the basic facts of the offense should be cause for concern. Oversights may simply result from the multitude of factors in a particular case. On the other hand, deficits of information may signal an unwillingness on the evaluator's part to undertake the difficult, sometimes gruesome, work of centering the evaluation on the offender and his criminal acts. Therapy under these circumstances is not likely to be appropriately focused. Here, perhaps more than anywhere else, the reader should be vigilant for any tendencies on the part of the evaluator to minimize, overlook, or excuse the offender's acts.

What follows the offense is significant as well. An offender's actions after an offense often reveal how he attempted to conceal the offense or deflect blame onto others, including the victim. For example, an offender may project responsibility for his crime on the victim. Such projection often exacerbates the victim's trauma. The offender might tell the child not to tell, not to share their secret, or he may threaten the child if she tells. Another offender may express guilt and remorse and promise never to assault the child again (a promise that is seldom kept in practice). An offender may tell the victim to stop him from committing future assaults, implying that the offense was the result of the victim not being sufficiently clear about her intent. The child may even be punished for having allowed the assault to take place. Blaming the child for the incident inflicts additional psychological trauma.

Finally, there may be special circumstances relating to a particular case that are unique and whose importance is inescapable. For example, an offender may assault a child who has just experienced another extremely painful life event, such as the loss of a mother. Other examples might be the offender using weapons in a brutal way, offending against infants, or abusing a position of trust such as caretaker in a home for the developmentally disabled. Special circumstances should be highlighted in those cases where offenders showed a callous insensitivity to their victims.

Other Deviant Behaviors

In addition to describing the offense that led to a referral for evaluation, the therapist needs to explore other sexual offenses and related behaviors. Recent research suggests that there are very few offenders who only develop one form of deviant outlet (Abel et al., 1983).

In the evaluation process, the therapist must always keep an open, scrutinizing mind to the possibility that other deviant behaviors have occurred. It is not uncommon, for example, to discover that an offender who engaged in sex without force with a 13-year-old child has also forced sex on other children and/or adults. The possibility of sex with animals, exposing, peeping, and other forms of sexual activity needs to be considered as well. The evaluator must make clear all the possibilities that were explored and the resulting information gathered. Failure to identify, discuss, and treat these other areas of deviancy allows the offender to believe that he can deceive the therapist. It also allows deviant patterns of behavior to remain intact, which may set the stage for future offending.

The Offender's Perspective

Corroboration of the incident through police reports and other evidence is essential. However, the offender's statement may also yield important information. If the offender denies, distorts, or minimizes his responsibility in the offense, his statement provides a perspective that is useful in understanding him.

One offender may freely acknowledge the extent of his offending, including information a victim was reluctant or unable to provide. Another offender will deny even the obvious, or claim that he cannot recall what occurred because of alcohol, drugs, or being otherwise unconscious of his actions. Most offenders will insist on the absolute truth from those who report about them and tend to complain that the victim's report is totally flawed if she errs in even one aspect of her statement.

The therapist's report should indicate the clarity and completeness of the offender's perspective by identifying the offender who talks openly and readily answers all questions about how he accomplished his crime as well as the offender who only gives the briefest detail. How much detail an offender willingly provides may indicate his amenability to therapy. When a therapist must spend much time in therapy teaching a client how to talk openly and honestly about his offense, less time remains to spend on the other tasks of therapy (i.e., reducing deviant arousal patterns, teaching empathy for others, teaching methods for controlling angry impulses, and so on), or therapy is greatly prolonged.

After describing the offender's view of the crime, the evaluator should discuss discrepancies between the offender's perspective and the other accounts of the crime. The therapist should highlight rather than dismiss such discrepancies. Possible reasons for such discrepancies should be discussed, and the implications they may have for the evaluation and for therapy should be noted. For example, an offender who completely denies the victim's and witnesses' statements, alleges that they have conspired against him to retaliate for other deeds, or claims that he has neither personal nor sexual problems is not likely to invest himself in therapy.

At times, discrepancies may not be so obvious. There may be total or near total agreement between the offender and the victim. An offender may admit to fondling a child's vagina but deny penile penetration when penetration is known by other means to have actually occurred. There are often good explanations for such discrepancies: The offender may clearly realize that he is out of control and needs help, but he may also figure that it is either too embarrassing or too risky to admit to the full extent of his deviancy, so he admits the lesser offense and denies the greater one. When discrepancies exist, the therapist should identify and discuss them. He or she must come to a conclusion about what to believe, as what the therapist believes will have an important bearing on the course of therapy. If a therapist believes that the victim was actually seductive and actively sought sex with the offender, treatment is more likely to focus on personal judgment and self-restraint in the face of temptation. On the other hand, if the therapist believes that the act was predatory and coercion or force was used, the course of therapy would be dramatically different.

The reader has a right to know where the therapist stands on such discrepancies. Judges, for example, have to make important decisions affecting the safety of the community. Given this responsibility, they must be certain that the therapist shares the court's basic understanding of the offender's criminal behavior. Failing to make the therapist's point of view clear increases the jeopardy faced by the community. Judges, prosecutors, and others are left making important decisions without benefit of the evaluator's informed opinion. Only the evaluator can make his or her viewpoint clear. The reader should not need to guess where the therapist stands on vital issues.

Denial, minimization, and rationalization are three characteristics that a careful evaluator describes. As noted, an offender who totally denies his offense is not likely to benefit from therapy. Likewise, an offender who minimizes or gives only token acknowledgment of having committed a crime will invest himself only superficially in therapy, unless the therapist is able to bring him to an attitude of more candor. An offender might be expected to justify, excuse, or otherwise rationalize his behavior, and the absence of these characteristics may be a favorable indicator. On the other hand, nondefensive candor about the details and extent of the abuse may indicate that the offender is so extremely asocial that he lacks the capacity to understand or care about the impact of his sexual assault. Judges and others reading the report need to know this information about the offender and the meaning the evaluator attaches to it.

Lack of truthfulness by the offender can be more serious, depending on the degree to which accounts are discrepant. Few therapists contend that they can be certain of all aspects of an offender's history and personality. In cases of total denial or of explanations at odds with victims' accounts, polygraph tests can often shed light. (For further discussion of polygraph examinations, see the section "Test Results.")

Another aspect of the offender's perspective is his ability to empathize. The report should illustrate how well the offender is able to understand the victim's experience. Does the offender relate to another person's physical and psychological pain? Can the offender appreciate the harm that he has caused? The offender's empathy can be a barometer of how well he is able to internalize the lessons of therapy. To the extent that empathy is lacking, reoffense prevention will have to be strengthened through other means.

Caution should be used in exploring and describing an offender's empathy. The evaluator should not mistake the offender's own selfish and personal pain and suffering for empathy for the victim. Bright, well-educated offenders are often able to appear empathic; however, when questioned in more than cursory fashion, superficiality is often revealed. For example, an offender may say he is sorry for having committed his offense because it caused the victim a great deal of shame, embarrassment, and financial hardship. When the therapist asks, "What else?" such a client's well of responses often runs dry.

Having empathy means more than identifying pain or embarrassment in the victim. Empathy means having the ability to experience another's feelings as though they were one's own. The offender will not just be personally embarrassed or pained but will be able to see the consequences of his offending throughout the victim's life. It means knowing that the child, for example, has suffered academically in school, has learned to avoid intimacy, has distanced him- or herself from classmates and friends, has developed the belief that the world is an unsafe place, or has developed confused attitudes about sex and love.

It is rare to find an offender who has deep feelings about the harm inflicted on his victims. The offender who has some ability to empathize is more likely to accept responsibility for his behaviors, derive more benefit from treatment, and thus be less likely to reoffend.

When handled well, this section of an evaluation report will prove one of the most valuable to the reader. It will provide evidence to judge the dangerousness of an offender and his amenability to treatment. It will also allow the therapist to establish credibility and competence by handling a complex topic in an informed and forthright manner.

PERSONAL HISTORY AND SOCIAL FUNCTIONING

Offense behavior alone provides inadequate information to decide the best disposition in a case. A clear description of the offender's personal history and social functioning will help the evaluator to place the offense behavior into a manageable context for the reader and to recommend for or against community treatment as an alternative to inpatient treatment or incarceration. Several broad questions need to be answered in this process, including the following: Has this person demonstrated reliability in the past? How does this person confront and deal with problems? What internal and external factors might affect the outcome of treatment, either positively or negatively?

The therapist's evaluation of the offender should cover (a) family of origin; (b) military experience; (c) education, employment, and financial history; (d) marital history; (e) substance use and abuse; (f) mental health history; (g) medical history; and (h) criminal justice history. Although no report can conceivably cover all aspects of any person, these topics may prove significant in understanding the offender. In most cases, they should at least be covered in the evaluative process, if not discussed thoroughly in the report. Complete detail of an offender's background is more than can be expected in any report; however, there are important areas that should be discussed clearly. The therapist's judgment must guide the selection of events to be discussed. When an area is not covered, the reader must ask whether the information would alter the conclusion of the report if it were known and were included.

The positive aspects of the offender's history should also be included in the report. While strengths may be emphasized less, considering the purpose of the report, positive resources and accomplishments in the offender's life help explain overall functioning.

Family of Origin

Review of the offender's family of origin should include the basic family constellation during childhood, highlighting any significant problems that may have had an important influence on the offender's development. Child abuse, drug or alcohol abuse among other family members, and known mental health problems should be highlighted. Parental divorces and remarriages, new marriages, and common-law relationships may have laid the groundwork for establishing relationships in the offender's current life. The existence or lack of an extended family may help shed light on some of the dynamics of the current offenses. The degree of connectedness to the community as a whole can help the reader understand the cultural norms and experiences that may have shaped the offender's personality, pattern of offending, and potential response to therapy. Family norms and experiences can serve as guideposts in assessing the offender's progress and response to therapy. For example, an offender's leaving an extended family may be an indicator of breaking free of a dysfunctional family system, which he used in the process of victimization, or the offender's ejection from the family system. From this standpoint, it is important to recall that no event has a single meaning. Rather, any event must be understood within the context of the offender's life.

Military Experience

History of military experience can be valuable because it is often the first reflection of the offender's functioning as an adult outside the family home. Issues to look for include whether the offender completed his tour of duty, had disciplinary problems, or received anything less than an honorable discharge. Military service is often a person's first time away from home, with first access to alcohol, drugs, prostitutes, and other similar activities. Failure to successfully complete military service may foreshadow problems for completing therapy. Military service may have provided structure that the offender now lacks, or it may have caused or exacerbated some problems. For example, veterans experiencing Delayed Stress Syndrome may need to address that problem before sexual deviancy treatment can be effective.

History of military service may provide other information about sexual history, dating, and other aspects of adult life that should not be overlooked by the therapist. Special attention should be paid to sexual behavior during military service because these early adult experiences often shed light on the development of deviant sexuality. Some information regarding military service can be crucial to the total success of therapy. For example, attitudes toward military superiors may reflect how an offender will relate to therapists, probation officers, or others in authority.

Education, Employment, and Financial History

A review of the offender's education provides an indication of early social adjustment as well as academic performance. Dropping out of school may be associated with a variety of factors, including educational or learning deficits, severe home-life problems, financial hardship, and poor social adjustment. However, many sex offenders have excellent educational records. A review of education may reveal information that will help predict and successfully guide the course of therapy.

Employment history, like military service, can be a valuable indicator of how well an individual has adjusted to adult life. Brief, serial employment may indicate a pattern that will be repeated in therapy. Prior employment may also be an arena of past sexual offending. The therapist should consider whether current employment may contribute to reoffense or whether adequate safeguards can be established.

Our experience dispels the myth that sex offenders generally come from the ranks of the unemployed: They often have good employment histories. The nature of their employment history may be an indicator of their capacity to apply themselves in therapy.

A review of the ways the offender has managed financial responsibilities can be revealing. Special note should be given to a history of high indebtedness, failure to meet financial obligations, dishonest or illegal business transactions, and bankruptcies. This information can suggest the degree of honesty and the sense of responsibility with which the offender is likely to approach evaluation and treatment. It is also indicative of the ability to manage one's resources and of personal coping skills.

Financial history is a major indicator of personal stability, especially in terms of impulse control. It reflects the offender's general integration into society. Financial history may indicate the likelihood of whether an offender will remain in treatment or use financial excuses to drop out of treatment as soon as he is confronted with difficult, painful, or disturbing personal issues that he would rather not deal with.

Changes in employment around the time of evaluation or during the course of therapy should be investigated carefully. It is not uncommon for a person with a long history of good employment to have job-related problems and possibly be dismissed or quit, making continued therapy difficult or impossible. Lack of funds and employment are among the most common precipitating causes of offenders' dropping out of the evaluation process or therapy. A good evaluation will carefully consider whether employment or lack of funds will likely be an impediment to therapy.

Marital History

Marital history plays an important role in understanding a sex offender. The number of marriages, separations, reconciliations, children, common-law marriages, adoptions, and so on can, almost by themselves, make a statement about the offender's personal history. The likelihood is that the patterns in one marriage are repeated in another. The cautious evaluator, however, will make as few assumptions as possible but will take a careful history of each marriage. The therapist will not allow vague statements like "we grew apart" to stand by themselves, but will probe to determine what the offender means by such statements. The statement "we grew apart sexually" can have widely divergent meanings, depending on the offender who uses it. It is the therapist's careful interviewing and investigation that gives such statements meaning. The therapist will confront the offender who states that "we put sex on the back burner" to find out what the offender actually means, and will explore the attitudes of both partners toward sex.

All previous marital relationships should be explored because of their potential value in understanding the offender. The therapist's failure to explore all relationships carefully allows the offender to conceal an abundance of possible deviancies. Vague generalizations about past marriages contribute to an offender's successful manipulation of the therapist. Alternatively, the offender can flood the therapist with irrelevant detail, deflecting the focus of the evaluation. A therapist who conducts a careful evaluation will not be lured into neglecting significant events in the offender's life or be overwhelmed by irrelevant details.

To illustrate the value of investigating previous relationships, consider the case of the offender who had claimed a history of sexual deviance limited to his present marriage. The daughters from each of two previous marriages responded to an investigator's inquiries by indicating that he had sexually abused them until they had reached the age when they could leave home. Then the offender divorced each wife and entered into the next relationship.

Substance Use and Abuse

An investigation of the role that both legal and illegal drugs and alcohol play in an offender's crime, and life in general, is essential. These drugs are often disinhibitors. Their use may release latent urges and may also provide a ready excuse to offend. They may contribute to reoffense by impairing the ability of the offender to learn new thinking and behavior in treatment. They may also provide the offender with excuses to explain away the sexual nature of his offense. Many offenders will tend to lay the blame for their sex offense on drugs or alcohol. They may state that they never would have committed the crime if they had been sober. In part, they are correct. They tend to err by implying that alcohol or drugs exclusively made them do something against their nature. The usual case is that alcohol or drugs play only a single part (in a complex situation of many parts) in releasing a latent characteristic that offenders were more able to control while sober. Seldom, if ever, have we seen a case where we believed that simple abstinence was a sufficient response to control the offender and eliminate the risk to the community. The evaluation will need to assess the complex role drugs and alcohol played in the offense and in the offender's life, and identify appropriate remedies.

In cases where an evaluator does not feel competent to do a thorough assessment of substance abuse, a referral to an appropriate agency familiar with the dynamics of sexual offenders is essential. The evaluation report should lay the groundwork upon which others, especially judges, can determine whether adjunctive drug or alcohol treatment is warranted.

Mental Health History

It is important that the therapist explore the offender's history of mental health functioning. Any periods of chronic depression, hallucinations, paranoia, or suicidal gestures should be examined. Prior treatment experience should be explored carefully whenever it exists because of the role it may play in coloring the offender's current expectations. For example, the depth of self-examination in vocational counseling is different from that in psychotherapy. Where many therapy experiences have taken place, their outcomes may foretell the outcome of the current process. Finally, they may provide important clues for success in the current therapy endeavor.

Prior treatment experiences are also important because the offender can use those experiences to learn the talk of therapy, anticipate the therapist's questions, and lead the therapist into exploring areas that are of advantage to the offender, thus steering the therapist away from the offender's sexual deviancy. Without exploring the extent and nature of past therapeutic experiences, the evaluator can unwittingly be drawn into misconceptions about the offender.

Medical History

An offender's medical condition may play an important role in therapy. It is common for an older offender with a history of heart problems to claim that confrontive therapy may jeopardize his health. While such complaints may be manipulative at face value, they cannot be taken lightly. Medical illness and medication may have a bearing on sexual functioning, including one's ability to have an erection. In such cases, the report's value is limited if consultation with a physician is not included. The evaluation should clarify any claims by the offender that his health precludes his participation in elements of therapy.

Criminal Justice History

Knowledge of the offender's adult and juvenile criminal history is necessary. Criminal history includes both offenses that were officially reported and investigated by law enforcement agencies and incidents that may have never been reported. The evaluator will ask the offender, for example, about criminal activity he has engaged in that has never been reported. In this regard, a carefully conducted evaluation of the sex offender can result in new crimes being discovered and solved or new reports to child protection agencies.

There are several sources of prior criminal history available to the evaluator. The offender is a principal source, as are significant others. Another valuable source of prior criminal history is the presentence investigation report prepared by a probation officer. The probation officer has the legal authority to request and receive information from nearly all criminal justice agencies around the nation. Criminal record keeping is not consistent within and among all legal jurisdictions. Some counties report felony convictions to state agencies for central record keeping, but other counties do not. Furthermore, misdemeanor offenses are reported very inconsistently to central state criminal justice information agencies. For these reasons, it is essential that record checks be conducted in every state, county, and city an offender has lived in during his adult life. This may at first seem difficult; however, experience shows that such record checks on most offenders can be completed with fewer than ten inquiries.

The evaluation should explore both felony and misdemeanor arrests and convictions. Sometimes, serious crimes are reduced to less serious, misdemeanor offenses. An offender may have been arrested, but, for a variety of reasons unrelated to his culpability, not prosecuted. The evaluator should thoroughly explore the nature of contacts with the criminal justice system rather than simply rely on conviction data.

In summary, personal history and social functioning should highlight the major influences on an individual offender. The full description should place the offender and his offending behavior in a wider social context so that courts and other community agents can make better decisions. Although thoroughness is not fully achievable in absolute terms, the reader must be careful to assess whether omissions may be significant and whether sufficient corroborative material has been used as a basis for the report.

SEXUAL HISTORY

A clear description of the offender's present sexual deviancy may have been covered previously in the report. It is unlikely, however, that the full historical extent of his sexual deviance was covered while describing the offense behavior. It is essential that the report address itself specifically to sexual history in order to (1) identify the areas of sexual behavior that are related to past and potential offending and that must be addressed in therapy, (2) provide a perspective regarding the longevity and severity of the problems, and (3) indicate the amount of supervision necessary in each case.

Sexual history includes sexual behavior, fantasies, feelings, and all related aspects of sexual experience from the time of the offender's first recollection of sex up to the present. In this area of the report especially, the tendency of the therapist should be to include more rather than less information and to describe patterns of sexual behavior where they exist. Sexual behavior in early childhood may include rape or molestation of the offender by adults, older siblings, or peers. The history should include the offender's reaction to any such events rather than assumptions made about their impact. Offender-initiated childhood sexual behavior should be included as well, of both a consensual and a coercive nature. Earliest sexual experiences, whether alone or with another, may provide significant material regarding an offender's psychosexual development. An offender's sexual history also includes what he saw others do sexually and what he thought about it.

A catalog of the offender's sexual behaviors can be extremely important both to the court and to the therapist. This catalog should include homo- and heterosexual activities as well as activities involving animals and inanimate objects. Attention should be paid to locations and circumstances promoting sexual arousal. The evaluation should include an exploration of the history and frequency of masturbation and masturbatory fantasies, with particular attention paid to deviant and offense-reinforcing fantasy material. The relationship between coerciveness and arousal patterns should be explored. The therapist should describe peeping, exposing, cross-dressing, use of pornography, frottage, and any other forms of behavior that may be idiosyncratic but add to understanding the offender. Where such activities are not discussed explicitly, the therapist should state clearly that they do not appear to exist and identify the basis for such a conclusion.

Frequency of sexual activities and the offender's attitude about those activities should be covered explicitly and in depth. Although numbers may be unreliable in the strictest sense, they may help explain the pace at which an offender's deviant arousal pattern may be extinguished. Without some estimate on the therapist's part of the frequency of sexual activity, a simple catalog of sexual behavior is of limited value. If the therapist has reason to doubt the offender's account — the offender may appear to be over- or underestimating frequency — polygraph examination can address concerns as to conscious efforts to deceive.

If not covered previously, the therapist should carefully explore all relationships involving sexual activity and sexual fantasy. Marital relationships are certainly important, but other relationships may be equally so. These can include the use of prostitutes, sexual activities with relatives (including in-laws), casual relationships (one-night stands), and the means of engaging in these activities, such as predation, frequenting singles bars, tavern hopping, and acquaintance rape. Information about whether — and, if so, how — knowledge of extramarital affairs was kept from the spouse can be instructive.

Finally, this section of the report should include a clear description of the offender's current sexual behavior and functioning, if it was not covered previously. The evaluator should explore whether the offender uses deviant fantasies to maintain sexual arousal with his current sexual partner. All of the areas described above should be examined to determine whether or not they pertain to current relationships and behaviors. Overall, the more complete the detail, the more it will help the reader evaluate the offender's current threat to the community, the seriousness and extent of his sexual deviancy, and the degree of rigor that the court should expect of the therapist.

TEST RESULTS

Some discussion of the results of special testing should appear in the evaluation report, either in a separate section or discussed within the context of other areas. The tests most likely to be used for the purpose of these evaluations include personality assessments or psychological testing and polygraph and plethysmograph testing.

Psychological testing is most useful as a check to see whether those findings are consistent with other sources of information, including personal history, report of significant other persons, and so on. It can also be useful as a means of pointing out special problems not evident from other information sources. There does not, however, seem to be a reliable, testable profile for the typical sex offender. There have been some attempts to develop such a measure, and certain groups, such as institutionalized sex offenders, do have many characteristics in common, but there is a growing awareness that offenders are represented by a wide array of demographic and personality types. It is certainly not possible to point to a particular personality profile and say, "This person is psychologically incapable of committing a sex offense." Of particular value in these cases is noteworthy information about validity-scale findings. Offenders may attempt to present themselves as not having the shortcomings and problems that most people have and readily admit to. This attempt to look good to the therapist may affect scores on the various clinical scales. The offender's unrealistic view of himself or his attempt to subvert the testing is valuable information in its own right.

Polygraph testing is another valuable information source. It can also be the object of considerable controversy, especially around the question of its reliability. It is not an absolute test of truth, but it is most useful as another source of information to be compared with other data, with the evaluator looking for a consistent pattern. Some examples may be useful. Consider the case of the accused offender who has denied anything close to inappropriate sexual behavior and, in fact, presents himself as an unusually virtuous person with no history of irresponsible behavior. Information from other sources indicates a pattern of dishonesty in his business dealings, some previous arrests for or accusations of similar offenses, and the discovery of a lie about some specific matter in his personal history. A polygraph finding that he was showing deception when denying that he had committed the present offense is an additional bit of useful information.

Turning to another example, consider the case of an offender who, when initially confronted about the present offense, admitted to essentially the same behavior that the victim described. He denied any other victims or offending behavior, but indicated deception when tested on the polygraph on that issue. He then admitted to another incident involving another victim not previously reported, and a follow-up test showed that he was now being truthful when denying further incidents. Polygraph testing here helped round out the data base on the extent of the offense behavior and gave some corroboration to the offender's statement that there were no more unreported offenses. In both cases, the evaluation is more complete, and plans for treatment and control can be made with a broader data base.

It is important to keep in mind that the polygraph is effective in testing for what the subject thinks to be the truth or a lie at the time of the test. Again, however, it is not an absolute test of the truth. It is common for a subject to work through one or more test procedures as indicated above and then, later in the course of treatment, to recall events that would seem to contradict an earlier finding of truth. Rather than invalidating the polygraph testing, this tends to validate progress on the part of the offender, who is beginning to examine his past behaviors in the light of new information gained through the treatment process.

There are some issues of quality control that need to be considered when using polygraph results. Licensing of polygraph operators in some states can provide some measure of assurance. So can the polygraphist's participation in the American Polygraph Association, which promotes technical competence and standards. But beyond the question of general competence comes the need for the polygraph operator to have some specific experience and skill in developing and administering questions to sex offenders. The offender who has been sexually abusing a child, for example, may be able to test as truthful when answering "no" to the question, "Have you been molesting your daughter?" He has, as part of the faulty reasoning that he used in giving himself permission to engage in that behavior, imagined himself to be providing useful sex education rather than engaging in any assaultive behavior. Thus polygraph testing for these offenders needs to incorporate explicit, specific descriptions that leave less room for the person being tested to make value judgments or interpretations of the meaning of behavior.

The penile plethysmograph is an electronic device used to measure the physical component of sexual arousal. It measures penile circumference with a small gauge that the client slips over the shaft of the penis. The client is introduced into a private setting, instructed on how to slip on the strain gauge, and then presented with a variety of sexual stimuli, such as audio tapes, slides, and so on. The changing circumference of the penis is measured by the plethysmograph and recorded. There is no pass or fail result in the use of this procedure. Rather, its most useful application is to measure the amount of arousal to one set of stimuli compared with arousal to other cues. Inferences can be made about the degree of attraction to offense or deviant stimuli when compared with more appropriate stimuli.

For example, consider the case of a man accused of sexual abuse of preadolescent boys. He admits to some inappropriate horseplay, but denies any sexual interest in boys. He states that his only sexual interest involves intercourse with his wife. Plethysmograph results indicate high arousal to boys, somewhat lower arousal to preadolescent girls, and almost no response to adult female cues. These results are very useful for the purposes of treatment planning and risk assessment. Comparing this data with other information would suggest that the man either is not truthful about his sexuality or is quite self-deceiving. He may have an active sexual relationship with his spouse but may be fueling his arousal with fantasy material involving minor males.

CONCLUSIONS AND RECOMMENDATIONS

Finally, most thorough evaluation reports will end with a section summarizing the most important issues discussed in the body of the report. This is important not just for purposes of good form and composition but because it is quite possible that this will be the only part of the report that some judges or parole board members may ever read. Thus it is useful to review those issues most important in making recommendations about supervision and treatment. Issues that deserve this sort of special attention should include the following:

(1) history of offenses and deviant behavior
(2) deviant arousal patterns
(3) defensiveness versus truthfulness: the extent to which the offender is taking responsibility for the offenses
(4) substance abuse or other problems needing adjunctive treatment or attention
(5) noteworthy testing results
(6) history of follow through and ability to observe rules
(7) history of inclination to violence or aggressive behavior
(8) medical or mental health problems

This section is most valuable as a review of both the resources and the risk factors the offender presents. Some mention of family and social supports, learning skills, and ability to empathize with others, especially the victim, can be useful in rounding out the picture of the offender. A formal diagnosis using the format of the *Diagnostic and Statistical Manual of Mental Disorders* (American Psychiatric Association, 1987) can also be used. However, that format is not likely to mean much to those who are not professional psychotherapists. Because this evaluation may well be the basis on which others will determine legal and community-safety issues, that diagnosis alone will not be very useful.

Most evaluations will end with some specific recommendations for treatment planning and those external controls that should be applied for purposes of risk management. The recommendations should logically follow from the summary and conclusions. If risk factors are identified, they should be addressed with specific recommendations about how to manage them. Below we have listed some typical recommendations for conditions of community-based treatment. The conditions are common starting points for such a program and should change only with the express prior approval of all the interested parties (including the community supervision agent) and when there is some reason to believe that the situation requiring these conditions has undergone a change.

This final section may also address any areas of special concern or reservations that the evaluator may have. For example, the offender may have some history of not following rules and may have contacted the victim by phone, contrary to the conditions of a court order to have no contact with her. He may be apparently repentant about this and express a willingness to follow the rules from now on, but the evaluator may want to highlight this as a potential problem area. The report may also set up contingencies, for example, to state that any such further rule violations will require the imposition of additional structure (such as work release) or demonstrate the need for institutional treatment.

TREATMENT CONDITIONS

The following are some typical conditions for community-based treatment. This list is certainly not exhaustive but it illustrates the specificity and thoroughness required to restrict offenders' behaviors and to provide for community safety. Each individual offender's circumstances should determine what conditions are needed in his case. Thought and concern should be given to tailoring conditions to suit each individual's needs.

General Conditions

(1) You shall enter and complete specialized treatment of sexual deviancy with (specific) agency and follow all relevant treatment rules.

(2) You shall be financially responsible for your own treatment and keep your account current.

(3) You shall take periodic polygraph and plethysmograph examinations as directed by the therapist.

(4) You shall be financially responsible for any treatment required by your victim(s).

(5) You shall have no contact with your victim(s) without the express prior approval of your therapist and community supervision agent.

(6) You shall lead an alcohol- and drug-free life-style. All prescription medications must be reported to your therapist and community supervision agent.

(7) You shall participate in an alcohol- or drug-abuse treatment or recovery program (as applicable) and submit to urinalysis or breathalyzer monitoring as directed.

(8) You are to use no sexually explicit material or to frequent establishments whose primary business pertains to sexually oriented or erotic material.

(9) You are to avoid situations or locales (specified) associated with prior offending.

Conditions Pertaining to Offenses Against Children

(1) You shall reside in a setting where there are no minor children.

(2) You shall hold no employment that places you in contact with or control over minors.

(3) You shall have no contact with any minors without the supervision of an approved adult chaperone who is fully informed of your offenses and behavioral rules.

(4) You shall not date, live with, or otherwise align yourself with any woman with minor children without the express prior approval of your therapist and community supervision agent.

(5) You shall not enter the family residence/property at any time without the express prior approval of your therapist and community supervision agent (for intrafamily abuse, offender out of the home, victim living at home).

(6) You shall not become involved as a supervisor, instructor, leader, or participant in any youth-oriented organizations.

(7) Reunification with your family (in cases of intrafamilial abuse) is dependent on the participation of your spouse in your treatment.

Conditions Pertaining to Establishing New Relationships

(1) You shall fully inform your potential partner ahead of time of your offenses with pertinent history and legal and treatment status.

(2) You shall inform your partner ahead of time of any sexually transmittable diseases you may have.

(3) You shall discuss with your therapist your intent to escalate your relationship.

(4) Your partner must join in your treatment program if your therapist deems it appropriate.

(5) You shall not be currently engaged in any other sexual relationships.

Chapter Six

Treatment Issues, Methods, and Measures of Effectiveness

Having explored some underlying assumptions about community-based treatment of sex offenders, the basic qualifications necessary for the therapist who would undertake such a practice, and the evaluation process, we will explore here just what should take place throughout the course of treatment. Of course, a thorough evaluation is necessary to set reasonable treatment goals. Particular goals will often be outlined in the conclusions of the evaluation report. Treatment issues are presented here in the order in which they generally should be addressed, with more critical issues first.

CONTROLS

The first issue of treatment is to ensure, in cooperation with community supervision agents, that sufficient external controls are in place to reduce the likelihood of reoffense. It is important to remember that offenders are not restricted by normal social and moral constraints. In fact, they are out of control in the sexual area and are poor predictors of their own future behavior. The therapist should work in a cooperative effort with others to impose and monitor clearly defined boundaries and behavioral controls. The nature of these controls will depend on, among other things, the nature and extent of the client's offense history, the sorts of situations he has been involved in, the victims he has preyed upon, and his demonstrated ability to follow rules. The wider and more serious the presenting behavior, the wider the net of external controls that needs to be applied.

The treatment conditions listed at the end of the previous chapter describe minimum controls that should be implemented at the beginning of treatment. These rules should include prohibiting access to primary victims and potential victims. For example, an offender who has assaulted a child within the family should have no contact with that victim, nor should he have any unsupervised contact with any children. Chaperones for these situations should be responsible adults who have a thorough understanding of the offender's sexually deviant history and are willing to help him maintain the necessary behavioral controls when he is in the presence of children. Exhibitionists (exposers) or voyeurs (peepers) should have their schedules structured so that they do not go cruising for opportunities to reoffend. There should also be prohibitions against the irresponsible use of chemical disinhibitors, and offenders with an alcohol- or drug-abuse history should be prohibited from any consumption of that substance. Parallel participation in alcohol- or drug-abuse treatment may also be appropriate.

The therapist should be part of a team effort to monitor the existing controls to see that they are sufficient and are being followed. This treatment/supervision team not only includes the therapist and the community supervision agent (such as the probation officer) but also may involve various family members and the offender's minister, employer, and friends. Of course, the therapist will need to obtain the written consent of the offender-client to permit the sharing of information with these other people. In addition to obtaining the offender's self-report, spot checks should be made. Therapists and others should check with family members and the therapist treating the victim of intrafamily abuse to see if their report of compliance matches the offender's. Polygraph testing with questions about whether the offender has broken any rules is another data source. Urinalysis tests to check for the presence of any prohibited chemicals are often helpful.

During the course of treatment, as offenders demonstrate the capacity to develop and exercise more internal controls, external controls can be modified accordingly. On the other hand, if the initially imposed controls are not sufficient to prevent infractions, then increasingly stringent controls should be applied. It has been our experience that many problems are avoided by taking a conservative stance at the beginning of treatment, imposing significant external controls to start up, then modifying them as offenders demonstrate a capacity to act responsibly with less stringent rules. It is much more complicated, and the associated risks are too great, to do it the other way around.

DEFENSES

Having established a layer of external controls around the offender, the therapist can begin to help the offender make the internal changes needed to prevent reoffense in the long run. The first issue is addressing the offender's defenses. Offenders are typically resistant to acknowledging the full nature and extent of their sexually deviant and antisocial history. One defense mechanism is denial, where the offender simply states that something didn't happen. For example, he denies having committed any offense and says the victim is lying, others misunderstood what happened, and so on. This must be resolved before any change process can begin.

Another defense mechanism, minimization, is more subtle. An offender may say that he did some, but not all, of what he is accused, or he may project some or all of the responsibility on someone else. He may say the victim encouraged his sexual attention, or that his wife drove him to the offense behavior by her lack of interest in continuing a sexual relationship on his terms. He may justify or rationalize his offenses: The child molester may define his behavior as sex education; the exhibitionist may insist that it was an accident that he was seen while he was exposing.

Treatment can begin only when offenders believe that there is, indeed, a problem. Treatment must focus on helping offenders acknowledge (a) that the problem has to do with their behavior, (b) the harm it has caused, and (c) the way in which they gave themselves permission to behave in that way. Dealing with defense mechanisms requires that the therapist confront those defenses and point out the errors and inconsistencies. This confrontation needs to be direct, with the offender hearing that what he is saying is not credible. The therapist can say that he or she understands that the offender has many reasons to try to persuade others that the nature and extent of his problem behavior are less than they really are. Nevertheless, the treatment process cannot proceed until the offender is dealing with his offense in an open and honest way. Group treatment is a particularly effective tool to use in this process because offenders can confront one another's defenses, often listening to each other in a way that cannot occur with a therapist alone.

The first measure of an offender's defenses being reduced is his report of the presenting offense behavior matching that of the victim and other witnesses. Scrupulous honesty is a major treatment goal, and the more that offenders seem to be honest, the better. But, as in all matters of this sort, the therapist must seek out corroborating sources of information to compare with the offender's self-report. Offenders often begin by giving lip service to accepting responsibility for their behavior but will still excuse the behavior when talking with friends or family members. They may only be able to talk about their responsibility in the most superficial way and be unable to understand the damage caused by the assaults to the primary victim and to other family members (secondary victims). Polygraph and plethysmograph testing should be conducted to see if those results are consistent with what offenders say about their antisocial and sexual history.

DEVIANT SEXUAL AROUSAL

The next major area that must be addressed in specialized treatment of sex offenders is the client's sexual behavior, thoughts, feelings, and fantasies. This gets to the core of the attraction to the offense behavior. Nearly all offenders have some significant degree of arousal to deviant stimuli (Marshall, Barbaree, & Christophe, 1986; Murphy & Barbaree, 1988; Quinsey, Chaplin, & Carrigan, 1979). Many offenders are significantly more aroused to deviant sexual stimuli than they are to more appropriate sexual cues (Barbaree & Marshall, 1989). That is why they risk going to jail in order to engage in their offending behavior. Treatment for sex offenders must include identifying existing stimulus and arousal patterns, including a thorough exploration of sexual fantasy and imagery. Offenders will typically underestimate the degree of arousal they obtain from offense-related stimuli, or they will state that since they have been apprehended there is no longer any interest in sex of any kind. There is often a suppression effect following disclosure of the offending when offenders may go through a monastic period in which they avoid sexual behavior of any kind. However, this is likely to be short-lived, followed by a return to previous sexual interests. Deviant patterns of arousal should be expected. A baseline of deviant sexual arousal should be established early in treatment. This provides a benchmark against which progress in reshaping sexual arousal can be measured.

There are a variety of methods used to reshape and reduce deviant arousal and enhance appropriate arousal. Most use behavioral and cognitive shaping. Nearly all require that offenders keep track of their sexual thoughts, feelings, fantasies, and behaviors, and avoid doing those things that would reinforce or sustain an interest in deviant sexuality. An absolute prohibition on masturbating to deviant fantasies should be implemented. The external controls, mentioned earlier, serve to reduce access to deviant sexual stimuli and opportunities to act on and reinforce deviant sexual impulses.

Covert sensitization is one behavioral method useful in reducing attraction to deviant stimuli. Through the use of guided imagery, the therapist has the offender imagine specific deviant behaviors. Instead of this leading to a pleasurable outcome, as it has in his previous fantasies or in his offending behavior, in this situation the therapist has the client imagine it leading to unpleasant consequences, such as going to prison. Olfactory conditioning uses a similar process, pairing the image of the deviant behavior with a disgusting smell. Guided imagery techniques can also be used to reinforce arousal to appropriate sexual stimuli.

It is important to recognize that, when pursuing pleasure from deviant behavior, offenders are driven by the arousal and do not see the behavior clearly. Masturbatory reconditioning can be used both to reinforce arousal to appropriate sexual cues and to reduce arousal to deviant sexuality by having offenders look at the behavior from a nonaroused state. Here they are directed to create an appropriate sexual fantasy and masturbate, using that fantasy, to ejaculation. Then, in the nonaroused state, they verbalize deviant sexual behaviors or masturbate to those fantasies with a flaccid penis for a preset period of time. Pairing nonaroused, unsatisfying sexual activity with the deviant fantasy helps them see the role of that fantasy in their behavior, resulting in their finding it increasingly unattractive. Masturbating to appropriate thoughts and scenes encourages them to see that there are other, more appropriate, and increasingly attractive alternatives.

Another method to help offenders understand more clearly the nature of their deviant behavior is modified aversive behavior rehearsal. Here the offender role-plays his offending behavior, using manikins. This can be videotaped and replayed for the offender and his spouse or significant others to view. This experience can dramatically strip away pleasurable illusions about the deviant fantasies.

For offenders experiencing hypersexuality, behavioral controls limiting the amount and nature of sexual activity are often imposed. For some, hormonal treatment (most notably, use of Depo-Provera) can be prescribed to reduce out-of-control sexuality and to provide some time for behavioral methods to begin to take effect.

Whatever method is employed, the end result of treatment should be the reduction of deviant sexual arousal and the reinforcing of appropriate arousal. The measures of success of this part of treatment should include a reduction in the offender's self-report of deviant fantasies, impulses, and behaviors. That self-report should be corroborated by other sources of information. Those sources include plethysmograph testing, a physiological measurement of sexual arousal discussed in more detail in Chapter 5. Barbaree and Marshall (in press) have reported that the posttreatment level of deviant sexual functioning plays a significant role in determining the likelihood of reoffense. Polygraph testing to check the offender's self-report is also helpful, as is consultation with the offender's spouse or significant others to discuss improvements in appropriate sexual functioning and related changes in behavior and living patterns.

COGNITIVE DISTORTIONS

Errors in the offender's thinking that have supported his deviant behavior should be dealt with in treatment. Denial, minimization, rationalization, justification, and projection of responsibility — the defense mechanisms described above — are all cognitive distortions. As treatment progresses, other, more global thinking errors need to be confronted and changed. An example is objectification, where the offender sees other people as objects that are either obstacles in his way or objects to use for his pleasure. Offenders also typically want power and control, believing that they must have what they want when they want it. Paradoxically, they often feel helpless and victimized, unable to get what they believe they need to survive. This belief that they are victims is another cognitive error that needs to be confronted and changed. Because offenders typically focus attention on their own feelings of helplessness, they seldom have an appreciation for the effect of their behavior on others.

Treatment for offenders should include identifying and confronting these thinking errors so that cognitive reshaping can take place. Offenders need to develop a sense of personal responsibility and concern for others. Without these changes, offenders are likely simply to be more cautious about not getting caught in the future rather than being more concerned about the consequences their behavior has for others. Group treatment is an especially useful tool for this purpose.

One of the measures used to see if these changes are taking place is monitoring the offender's belief statements in the therapy sessions. This would include statements of personal responsibility (including a willingness to be open and honest about personal shortcomings) and concern for others. Checks should be made to see whether the offender is applying these changing beliefs to his relationships with family members and significant others. In general, as the offender makes improvements in this area, the quality of life of those closest to him should improve also. Polygraph testing can also be used to check whether the offender is being truthful about following treatment conditions; it may indicate changed beliefs and attitudes.

DEVELOPING SOCIAL SKILLS AND SUPPORTS

In the later stages of treatment, a variety of issues can be addressed that have to do with improving the general quality of life of offenders: helping them develop and maintain healthy adult relationships, deal with frustration, and so forth. Most general practice mental health professionals are most familiar with this area of therapy and, due to their lack of experience with sex offenders, would be likely to begin treatment of offenders here.

The typical offender enters treatment expecting that these are the areas most likely to be covered, resulting in his being happier and feeling better about himself. He is typically quite disturbed to find that, rather than having his ego massaged, he must begin by following strict external rules and having his justifications for his behavior confronted. The therapist is likely to experience this as more like parenting an unwilling child than like therapy.

Eventually, because sex offenses are committed in the pursuit of pleasure, part of the treatment should involve helping offenders find appropriate alternatives to their deviant behavior. To be sure, responsible behavior will probably never provide the excitement of offense behavior, but offenders should have alternatives that are reasonably available if they are to refrain from reoffending and forsake the pleasure they would derive from it. Offenders often use sex, and especially deviant sex, to solve myriad life problems. Sex is often used as a means of reducing tension, as a sedative to aid falling asleep at night, or as the first, and often only, factor to take into consideration when developing relationships with women. Social and coping skill training may be necessary for some offenders in order to assist them to broaden their range of appropriate social functioning. In a few cases, offenders may require some basic sex education. Assertiveness training can help some to develop skills to express what they want in nonaggressive, nonmanipulative ways and to broaden their sense of empowerment and reduce the temptation to feel helpless and victimized. These men need to understand that they have choices, but they also need to have some ability to make those choices and follow through on them. The way they relate to their spouses and other members of their families often needs to be addressed in couple and family counseling.

The measure that changes are taking place in these areas should include the client's self-report of developing and improving primary and secondary relationships with appropriate peers. As always, these self-reports should be compared with the reports of others in the offender's social circle.

In summary, it is our belief that, because the most important goal of specialized treatment of sex offenders is to prevent reoffense both during and after treatment, those issues most likely to contribute to that goal should be addressed first. We have presented the various treatment issues in roughly the order in which they should be addressed in treatment. To be sure, there will be a good deal of overlap. Challenging cognitive distortions, for example, will begin long before offenders have completed making the necessary changes in their deviant sexual arousal system. However, unlike more traditional therapy with voluntary clients, where improving self-esteem and a sense of empowerment are important prerequisites of change, the issues in this last section should not be the first priority when treating sex offenders. In most cases, the offender should not be encouraged to feel better about himself until he has begun to make the significant changes necessary to reduce the likelihood of reoffense.

OTHER INDICATORS OF APPROPRIATE TREATMENT

Here we will outline some general indicators that appropriate treatment is taking place. First of all, the therapist must recognize that cessation of offending is of paramount importance and takes precedence over all other considerations. Although this may seem obvious, it needs to be emphasized because of its implications for therapy and the role treatment plays in protecting community safety. Indications that this principle is being followed include the imposition of clear and strong behavioral rules (see Chapter 5 for examples) and the therapist's statements about treatment, reports to court, and willingness to consult with others about the case. Offenders will object to the wide range of disruptions to their life that result from this approach and will likely test limits as they are imposed. These are not men, however, who can or will set their own limits, and the therapist must be willing to be part of a team that sets external controls.

The person who commits sex offenses has serious problems that involve many areas of his life, requiring intensive and often lengthy treatment to affect the substantial changes required. The therapist treating such a client should recognize this, and plans for treatment should be in accordance with this understanding. Thus appropriate treatment will be comprehensive and take a good deal of time to complete.

An appropriate therapist should recognize that primary and secondary victims (to include all other family members) have treatment needs of their own (see Chapter 2, "A Primer on Victimology"). These needs should be addressed by someone with experience and expertise in working with victimization. This is another specialty area and should not be attempted by the mental health generalist. Furthermore, the incest victim needs to see her therapist as supportive and as an advocate for her interests alone. The problems the victim faces are clearly different from the offender's. This needs to be explicitly stated and demonstrated by having a specialist help the victim with her concerns. The victim needs to hear that she is not the cause of the offense, not the reason for the disruption in the family life, and not the reason that the offender is in trouble with the authorities. The victim should not be expected to sacrifice her need to feel safe and comfortable in order that the offender may return home. The victim specialist acts as a proponent for the needs of the abused child and will advocate for things that will conflict with the desires, and even best interests, of the offender. *This cannot take place when a single counselor is the primary therapist for the offender, the victim, and the family as a whole.* Before any attempt at family reunification is made, the needs of primary and secondary victims should be addressed in separate, specialized treatment (see Chapter 7, "Reuniting Incest Offenders with Their Families").

The therapist working with the sex offender should be available and willing to work in cooperation with other parts of the community supervision team. This cooperation should include, at a minimum, that the therapist will immediately report if the offender violates *any* rules.

The offender should be able to describe what is occurring in treatment. This is unlike much nondirective talk therapy, where it may be difficult to put into words what is taking place during the counseling sessions. In specialized treatment for sex offenders, the issues described above should be specifically addressed, and the client should be able to relate to this course of treatment in a fairly clear way. For example, he should be increasingly clear about the thinking errors and behaviors that he made and that were part of the process leading to the assaults. He should be able to give specific examples and also to identify areas on which he still needs to work.

Appropriate therapy will permit the community supervision agent to see, during the course of treatment, the offender assuming increasing personal responsibility. He should be able to talk more directly about his offenses, the harm they caused, and what specific steps he is taking to reduce the risk of reoffense. It should begin to be apparent that the offender, rather than others, is taking the initiative to broaden the foundation of his behavioral and social controls. Examples of this would include his informing others about his offenses and the behavioral rules he must follow. The offender should begin, over time, to arrange things so that the sometimes inconvenient nature of these rules not be a burden for others.

CONTRAINDICATORS

There are also some contraindicators that suggest that appropriate, offense-specific treatment is not taking place. A therapist who is not interested in working in cooperation with other community supervision agencies probably does not recognize that the offender needs a team of external agents to put external controls in place and monitor them. There can be no busy schedule or other excuse that would result in the therapist being unwilling to provide periodic progress updates or appear in court to testify if requested. (Community treatment should not be offered to offenders who are unwilling to release their therapist from client-therapist confidentiality restrictions.) Similarly, the therapist who does not seek independent sources of information to compare with the offender's self-report shows no appreciation of the offender's inclination to withhold or minimize relevant facts.

Treatment that fails to address the five specific treatment issues described above, fails to deal with sexual matters, or is not substantially confrontive is probably not going to be effective in preventing reoffense in the long run. If the therapist allows the offender to sidetrack treatment to address tangential issues, then offense-specific therapy gets lost. Likewise, if the therapist is unwilling to make the client uncomfortable by confronting his behavioral and thinking errors, appropriate treatment is not taking place.

Another contraindicator is when a therapist fails to confront not only the behavior involved in the referring problem but a whole range of supporting behaviors. These may include failure to meet financial, family, and work responsibilities, irresponsible pleasure seeking, such as substance abuse or gambling, or controlling others through anger outbursts. Any violations of legal or treatment requirements should be confronted and reported, as should any return to sexually deviant patterns. A therapist who apologizes in any form for the offender's behavior is certainly a contraindicator.

TREATMENT FAILURES AND TREATMENT SUCCESS

Offenders enter treatment with a number of significant problems that need to be addressed. They bring an array of behavioral and thinking patterns that will need to be changed. Because of the attraction to the offense behavior and their characterological defects, offenders require substantial external controls. Because they will tend to test those controls, the boundaries established by these rules should allow for a reasonable margin of safety. The slightest deviation from the rules or crossing of the established boundaries should be confronted and incorporated into the treatment process. This should, over time, result in some observable changes in behavior and thinking. If, however, an offender persists in his old patterns of behavior and continues to test the limits and to engage in irresponsible behavior, the team supervising his community-based treatment, including the therapist, should begin to ask whether more structure or more intensive treatment is required.

Community-based treatment should only be offered for those sex offenders who are able to make the changes necessary to prevent reoffense over the long run. Some offenders are obviously not appropriate candidates for outpatient treatment. Others, however, may appear amenable to community treatment and begin therapy, but over time they may demonstrate that they are not making progress. It is reckless and irresponsible to continue to keep in treatment and discharge as a treatment success any sex offender who does not make the needed changes. Successful completion of community-based, sex-offense-specific treatment should be viewed as a minimal requirement. It is the least intrusive intervention along a continuum that includes inpatient treatment and long-term incarceration. If an offender cannot or will not change in the outpatient setting, a more restrictive alternative should be imposed. The therapist and others on the community supervision team must recognize the limits of their capacity to help offenders change. Treatment failures do occur and should be anticipated. When they occur, the supervision/treatment team should recognize the failure, have alternative responses available, and be willing to implement them. Sex offenders who fail to successfully complete specialized treatment are high risks to reoffend (Barbaree & Marshall, in press).

The issue of treatment success must also be viewed cautiously. Much in the same way that an alcoholic should never consider himself cured, so must the sex offender who completes treatment remember that his deviant behavior is only in remission. He has a behavioral and thinking handicap that he can keep within acceptable limits only by continuing to practice a series of controls. As he demonstrates increasing internal controls, external controls can be cautiously relaxed. Failure to remember the need to practice the lessons learned in specialized treatment sets the stage for possible reoffense. Sex offenders can go on to lead full, rich lives without reoffense. They can incorporate the necessary changes into their lives just as an alcoholic, a diabetic, or a person with a heart condition can. However, failure to do so can be catastrophic.

Chapter Seven

Reuniting Incest Offenders with Their Families

When therapists and criminal justice professionals find themselves working with a family in which child sexual abuse has occurred, a whole host of intricate problems are presented when the members of such a family wish to remain as a family. There may be conflicting goals in this situation. Reuniting the offender with his family could, for example, interfere with the healing process of the victim and distract the offender from the important issues he needs to deal with in order to prevent reoffense. This chapter will outline these issues and present a framework for working through them.

PRELIMINARY STEPS

Before discussing the process of reuniting families in which there has been sexual abuse of children by adults, we will outline some of the steps we believe should be taken when intervention and treatment first begin. As we have done in other chapters, we will be using as an example a generic situation with a female child victim and a father-figure offender. First of all, it is important that the offender be removed from the family situation and have no contact with the victim. This ensures the physical safety of the victim. Also of concern is the immediate and long-term emotional safety of the victim. Not only has the child suffered some significant upset as a result of the actual sexual abuse, there is significant trauma connected with the disclosure of this victimization. The victim has had a most private and intimate part of herself violated and an important bond of trust broken by the sexual abuse. It is most uncomfortable to have to report and recount these experiences. The victim often feels somehow guilty for having been selected for this abuse and feels that there must be something wrong with her. Add to this the feelings that come from knowing that the offender, someone for whom she may have some degree of affection, is getting into a great deal of trouble and the family is in an uproar, all seemingly because of her reporting the abuse.

In this very difficult situation, the victim should not have to deal with the offender and the possibility of his blaming her for the trouble he is facing, too. Even when the offender is admitting the abuse and responsibility for it, there is an inclination for him to feel depressed and ask forgiveness of the victim. The child may be pressured to excuse the adult and essentially deny the extent of the abuse. This more subtle form of revictimization can, of course, be accompanied by more dramatic pressures to accept responsibility for the sexual involvement or to recant her report in order to protect the family unit and the abuser.

Until a thorough assessment of the offender has been completed, including physiological testing to measure the extent of his sexual attraction to deviant sexual stimuli, he should not be in a position where he has regular contact with the source of his offense-related stimulation, the victim. He should not be in her presence until it can be determined that he is well along in the process of being able to control his sexual arousal in response to the child.

It is for such reasons that initially the offender should have absolutely no contact, either in person, by phone, or in writing, with the victim. This, of course, requires that he live in a separate residence. The preference is that the offender move from the family home and the victim remain. Berliner (1982) outlined some reasons for this preference:

(1) It is fairer to make the person causing the problem leave the home than the one who suffered the problem.

(2) It is a statement that adult offenders are responsible for their own behavior.

(3) Victims should be allowed to continue as normal a life as possible in their own family environment.

(4) It may help the family to focus on the victim's needs rather than on the needs of the offender.

(5) The general tension level in the home may be reduced when the offender is removed.

(6) Children have a right to be safe in their own home.

(7) Losing the right to live in their own home can help offenders learn that there are consequences for their behavior.

(8) Removal from the home provides the offender with a strong incentive to change, if making those changes are a condition of his returning to the family.

(9) The mother, who usually sees herself as less competent and more dependent, may come to realize her strengths.

We believe that the offender should have no contact with any minors during the assessment process and through the first stages of treatment. Until a thorough evaluation has been completed, the therapist does not know the full extent of the deviancy, the potential for predation, or the degree of compulsiveness in the offending behavior. Following a complete evaluation, this restriction can be modified as appropriate. One modification might be limiting contact with minors to situations where he is supervised by a responsible adult who is aware of his offenses and the behavioral restrictions he should observe when with children. The potential chaperone should meet with the therapist and be able to discuss the offense behavior, understand that it could recur, and be willing to intervene if the behavioral safeguards are not being observed. These behavioral rules include the following:

(1) The offender should never be alone with children without a chaperone present and on duty.

(2) The offender should never be responsible for supervising or disciplining minors.

(3) The offender should never initiate physical or affectional contact with minors.

(4) If the child wishes to make a gesture of physical affection, such as a hug or kiss, the offender's response should be modest and brief.

(5) The offender should avoid situations of physical contact with minors, such as tickling, horseplay, children on lap, and so on.

(6) There should be no secrets between the offender and minors.

(7) The offender should not discuss matters of sexuality or dating with minors.

(8) The offender should not present himself as wanting or needing caretaking or special affection from children.

If the offender has some interaction with nonvictim children in his family, efforts should be made that this not be done in a way that the victim is left out of family activities, is made to feel blame for restrictions or prohibitions, or is put in the role of outcast and thus further victimized. It will take some time before the offender may have contact with his victim. Not only is the prevention of reoffense at issue here but also ensuring that the victim has an opportunity to heal the emotional wounds of her victimization. She needs the full support of her mother (the nonoffending parent) as well as specialized therapy. Therapy and support from others should help the victim know that her story about the abuse is believed and that she will be protected from further victimization. She needs to be reassured that the abuse was not her fault, and she should have made major gains in resolving the impact of victimization.

The mother, too, has some special needs in this situation. The mother will often need support in accepting that the abuse *really did occur*. The mother may need help in fully understanding that the abuse was the offender's responsibility and not the child's or hers. She will need some support in deciding whether to continue in a relationship with the offender, understanding that she does have some choices in this matter, and, when she does make a decision, she should be clear about the reasons behind that decision. If she intends to try to rebuild her relationship with the offender and hopes to reunite the family, she will also need some assistance in understanding the offender's behavioral and thinking handicaps. She will need to learn how those handicaps will affect their relationship and what she must do to protect the victim and other children in the future.

The offender, of course, has some important things he must accomplish before beginning to reestablish any relationship with the victim or becoming reinvolved in family life. His offense behavior should be brought under control. This will initially require a substantial amount of external control of the sort mentioned earlier. Internal controls, including self-management of arousal to deviant sexual stimuli, should be falling into place. In his treatment, he will need to have shown substantial progress at being open and less defensive about discussing his offense behavior. He must be able to clearly acknowledge that the offenses took place and accept that he is the one responsible for his behavior. He should clearly understand that projecting blame on the victim or others would only continue to hurt them. He should have a thorough understanding of the harm he has caused to the victim(s) and not merely be ashamed about his behavior or focus on the inconveniences to his own life that have resulted from treatment and justice system intervention. The offender should be well on the way to confronting his own excuses, rationalizations, and justifications for his offense behavior. He should see the abuse for what it was, his manipulating the trust bond and hurting someone over whom he exercised power and control for the purpose of giving himself pleasure.

Obviously, accomplishing these therapeutic goals for all parties will take some time. It is important that these initial objectives be addressed and be well on the way to being met before attempting to pursue family reunification. Premature attempts to bring the family back together risk several problems. The offender may attempt to project the blame, and the victim or others may take responsibility and feel guilty for the problem he created. The mother will be distracted from her task of providing support to the victim by attempting to placate and reassure the offender. She and others will become confused about what needs take priority as the offender asks for or demands attention. The offender will be off the hook, having much of what he wants restored and with less reason to do the work and make the changes necessary to prevent reoffense and create a healthy family atmosphere.

REESTABLISHING CONTACT

When this preliminary work has been accomplished, it may be time to begin to reestablish some contact between the offender and his victim. (Because there are often criminal justice, child protection, and family court agencies involved in these cases, the therapists will need to be sure that all parties are informed of the offender's and victim's progress in treatment and approve of reestablishing contact.) The best way to begin this process is to have the offender write a letter to the child. This letter should include the offender's telling the child that he accepts responsibility for the offense and that she was not to blame for the abuse. He should acknowledge that the abuse has caused her some hurt and perhaps give some indication of his understanding of that: "It must have been difficult having to keep it a secret. I understand that you didn't like what I was doing to you. My not telling the truth right away must have made it even tougher." These are some examples the offender can use here. He should also help relieve any feelings of guilt the child might have by stating that she did the right thing by telling, having the abuse stopped, getting help for herself, and also helping him to get the treatment he needed.

There are some specific things the letter should avoid saying. The offender should not be asking for forgiveness. Of course, it is hoped that the victim will be able, through counseling, family support, and personal growth, to move beyond the trauma of the victimization. Forgiveness (i.e., being able to let go of the feelings of betrayal and anger) would be an indication of progress on that front. But that forgiveness should be something she comes to as a result of the healing of her emotional wounds, not something the offender should demand or ask for. The offender should also avoid saying things in this letter that would tend to make the victim feel sorry for him. She has enough work to do in healing her own wounds without the added burden of ministering to him. To put her in that position would be to continue the pattern of the abuse. (Offenders often use a "what's the matter, don't you love Daddy," posture as a lever to overcome resistance to the sexual exploitation.) Similarly, the letter should avoid telling the victim what to do or how to feel about the situation. "Don't feel bad," or even "don't feel responsible," reinserts the offender into a position of manipulating or controlling the victim's thoughts and emotions. The victim needs the reassurance that the offender won't be manipulating or controlling her in the future as he has in the past.

The writing of this letter is an excellent vehicle that can be used in the offender's treatment to help him review many important issues relating to his assaults. It is unlikely that his first draft of this letter will be appropriate. His therapist should prepare him for this and indicate that subsequent rewrites are opportunities for learning. The letters should not, of course, be written by the therapist; nor should the offender merely parrot or paraphrase the therapist's words. This naturally takes longer and has potential for frustration, for both the offender and his therapist. Nonetheless, some rich learning opportunities are available here if the process is approached as an educational experience. Not only can the offender learn about the problems with the wording of his letter, but he can also look at some of his underlying thinking errors. He can be reminded of his self-centeredness, especially when he is self-pitying rather than focusing on the hurt to the child. He may have difficulty in giving examples about how the child has been hurt by the experience. This can be pointed out as demonstrating his lack of empathy for others, a contributing factor in the offense process. There may be good examples of how he tries to reassert control in either overt ways or through subtle manipulations.

This letter is best read by the victim with her counselor and possibly her mother in attendance. This allows the child to use these support people to help her sort through how she feels about his message and what she wants to do in response. The child may want to write a letter in reply. She may not be sure how she wants to proceed and may require some time to decide. She may not believe that the offender is sincere about what he says in the letter. She may simply want to have nothing more to do with this man who caused her so much pain. These latter examples illustrate some of the problems experienced by the more severely damaged victims or by families with more complicated problems. Some of these problems may be resolved over time. Some may not. However, when all parties *are* ready to move on toward reconciliation, there are some specific steps that we believe should be taken.

FIRST VISITS

The next step is usually a meeting in person between the victim and the offender. The best place for this is in the office of the victim's therapist. This meeting would usually include the victim, her therapist, her mother, the offender, and his therapist. Of course, some preparation is required for this meeting. The child and her counselor will have talked about, first of all, whether the girl is truly ready for the visit and wants to proceed. She will also want to talk about how she expects it will go and what will be discussed. The therapist will want to see if the victim has any things she especially wants to talk about or any situations she especially wants to avoid. The offender will have worked with his therapist on how to say, in person, most of the things he expressed in the earlier letter and how to respond to questions the victim may have about those issues. It is important that the abuse be acknowledged and dealt with directly. The visit should not end with any unresolved questions about responsibility, harm done to the victim, or the child's right to be protected from such exploitation. It should also be established that, except for planned counseling sessions with the therapists present, future interaction between the offender and the victim will not involve discussions of sexual abuse. A final topic of this first meeting is a discussion of future visits.

This first visit may actually require several more such meetings in the office of the victim's therapist. If there are questions about, for example, whether the offender truly does accept responsibility for the abuse or indeed believes that the victim did the correct thing by reporting the assaults, then these should be discussed. Before visits outside the therapist's office occur, the offender should present the behavioral rules he will observe during those visits. This list of rules should be well worked out in advance. The offender should understand the reason for the rules, accept them as reasonable and necessary, and be able to present them to his family as *his* rules that he will take responsibility for observing. These rules will typically include the following:

(1) The offender will never be alone with the victim (or other children for that matter).

(2) Identify who will be the designated adult chaperone(s) for the offender when he is with the victim. This should be someone with whom the victim is comfortable and is able to talk with about the abuse. The chaperone will often be the nonoffending parent, but this person may not be appropriate at this time.

(3) The offender will in no way be responsible for disciplining the victim. He will not administer any punishment or rewards. Any gifts given to the victim will be done through the chaperone following prior discussion and approval of both therapists.

(4) The offender will not initiate any physical or affectional contact with the victim. If the child wants to, for example, offer a hug or kiss of greeting or parting, she can do so.

(5) The offender will need to minimize physical contact, even though initiated by the victim. Affectional gestures (as discussed in above) should be brief. The offender will refrain from other kinds of physical contact, such as tickling, horseplay, having her sit on his lap, walking hand in hand, and so on.

(6) The offender will have no secrets with the victim.

(7) The offender will not engage in discussions of sexuality, dating, boy-friends, and so on with the child.

(8) Any further discussions about the abuse will be done in a treatment setting with counselors present.

(9) Other special rules necessary to allow the child to feel comfortable are instituted because of particular circumstances of the case.

In presenting these rules and in the accompanying discussion, the offender should clearly understand and be able to communicate that these rules are necessary because of *his* particular handicaps of behavior and thinking. They are not a reflection of anything being wrong with the victim or the family. These rules may seem a bit awkward or inconvenient at times. The child may at some time wish that a particular rule be ignored. The offender needs to be clear that to do so would risk his reentering an offense cycle. The purpose of discussing the rules is to clarify guidelines that everyone understands and will observe. There should be no ambiguity. Clearly stated expectations should minimize the problem of being uncomfortable because one is not sure of what is going to happen. The line between permissible behavior and inappropriate behavior should be clear to all.

FAMILY OUTINGS

After the procedures mentioned above have been conducted, the offender, the victim, and other family members can begin to have some visits without the presence of a therapist, although a chaperon would, of course, be present at all times. These visits should gradually introduce new experiences so that everyone can get accustomed to each new situation before moving on to the next. The first of these visits should be time-limited and not too lengthy, perhaps two hours. It should take place in a public setting, involve something for everyone to do, and provide an opportunity for social interaction. Examples of such meetings include having a meal in a restaurant or going shopping at a mall. The family home should still be a place of safe refuge for the victim and should not be used for these early visits. The use of a public place provides a comfortable setting for the victim as compared with the setting for the offenses, which was often a private or out-of-the-way place. Going to a movie theater, often suggested for this first visit, is not advisable. No one will get a chance to interact, and one of the purposes of these meetings is to have the family members socialize and see what it feels like to be together.

It should be understood that these visits are trial affairs, and, if anyone (particularly the victim) is feeling uncomfortable about the way things are going, it is perfectly OK to end the visit. The child can tell the non-offending parent about her feeling uncomfortable. The mother can then inform the offender, and the visit will end gracefully, with no need for the victim to discuss the matter with the offender. There should be no expectation that the victim should suffer through an unpleasant experience. That is exactly what happened during the course of the abuse, and the purpose of treatment is to change those patterns. The offender should use separate transportation for these early meetings so as to make it easier to comfortably end the meeting and allow the victim to maintain some distance from him.

It is usually best to have an opportunity for the victim and the offender to meet with their respective therapists between these early meetings. This gives all parties an opportunity to discuss how the visits went, trouble-shoot any problems, and plan future outings. It is particularly important that the victim have an opportunity to discuss her feelings with her therapist. It is common that substantial pressure is applied to the victim, often in subtle ways, by other family members (including nonvictim siblings) to agree to allow the family reunification process to proceed rapidly. It should not be the victim's responsibility, however, to suffer through uncomfortable experiences to make this family reunification happen. The victim often needs to have available and be able to talk with an objective and informed person to help her sort through her feelings about these visits. If there are problems, they need to be addressed and corrected. If there are counseling issues that arise, these can be used in the therapy process. In any case, the reunification process is a delicate one that should proceed at its own pace and not be rushed through.

Having had several brief and successful visits, the family can then expand the range and scope of these meetings. The amount of time spent together could be increased gradually. The family could expand the range of places and activities. Semiprivate places such as the homes of relatives or friends could be used to spend time together. After several satisfactory visits, sharing transportation could begin, the offender and victim going and returning in the same car. As mentioned earlier, each of these new elements should be planned carefully, seeing that all goes well and everyone feels comfortable before adding yet another new factor.

At this point in the family reunification process, consideration can be given to making exceptions to the general plan for special occasions, such as holidays or birthdays. For example, meetings have been averaging two to five hours in length. There is an all-day affair planned for Christmas at Grandma's house. Plans can be made for such an exceptional situation, assuming that all parties feel they would be comfortable. It should be understood that Christmas is a special occasion and this get-together does not mean that all future visits will be all-day affairs. It should be noted that special events like Christmas or birthdays are not good times for first visits.

It should be expected that at various points in this process some problems will arise. Patterns of personal and family behavior do not change automatically. For the offender, these visits are a laboratory to test out new methods of thinking and acting with those closest to him. There will be relapses to old patterns, although it is hoped that with this gradual procedure those relapses will be minor and manageable. For example, the offender who has traditionally controlled his wife and children through fear by use of temper outbursts may throw a tantrum not directed at any person but about mechanical problems with the family automobile. Or the offender who had forged a special and secret relationship with the victim may commiserate with her out of earshot of the mother (nonoffending parent) after she has disciplined the child. These situations would be clear indications of offending patterns still being in place and needing further work. These examples should be addressed in the offender's therapy.

VISITS HOME

Assuming there has been continuing progress on the various issues as they arise and that everyone is comfortable with the idea, the next step would be to have the offender make some visits to the family home. This step should be taken realizing that the victim is losing her safe haven in the process. The offender should approach the family residence as a visitor rather than as someone who is returning to take charge and correct the problems that have developed in his absence. As with other major steps in the family reunification process, this one should be made with some planning. The first visit home should be fairly brief, with everyone knowing the schedule. This should be a time when there is some planned activity, not just an occasion when the offender hangs around the house. Having a family meal at home is a favorite way to use this time and usually works well for this purpose.

This is a new situation that requires some new rules so that everyone knows what to expect. In addition to the continuation of the rules for previous visits, these new rules should include the following:

(1) The offender should never enter the victim's bedroom. The child, who has relinquished the sanctuary of her home, thus still retains the bedroom as a safe haven.

(2) The offender should not be in any bedroom or bathroom with any children, even with a chaperone present.

(3) The practice of locking the bathroom door should be practiced by all members of the family (except for toddlers who may require the assistance of the nonoffending parent).

(4) Whenever possible, the offender should use separate bathroom facilities from those used by children, especially the victim. This again extends the safe haven concept.

(5) The offender should never be at the home when children are there, even if they are not in his immediate presence, unless a chaperone is also there.

(6) The offender should be fully and appropriately dressed at all times. The nonoffending parent is responsible for other members of the family being appropriately attired.

Assuming these early home visits go well (and the various therapists have had an opportunity to review them), the next step would be to have longer visits at home with somewhat less rigid structure. These visits often take the form of meals at home before or after an outing, or involve the offender in helping his spouse with household maintenance and repairs.

In this situation, the children often come and go, visiting with friends and engaging in their own activities apart from the adults. The family thus begins to interact and look more and more like a normal family. Regarding the friends and playmates of the children, if the offender is going to have more than an occasional and brief interaction with other children, the parents of those children should be informed of his offense and the behavioral measures (rules) he is following to prevent reoffense.

As always, making changes in this format and expanding the amount of the offender's involvement in family life should be done in a gradual, well-planned way. The earlier visits should be marked by the offender's avoiding being intrusive and learning how to fit into the family patterns, which will have changed some since the time of his offending and subsequent removal from the home. At these early visits, the offender should not plan on changing clothes or bathing at home, leaving that for a time when other issues of his reintegrating into the family routine have been resolved. The amount of time he will spend with his family will typically grow to include the better part of a weekend, except that he will not spend the night at home. If these visits are comfortable and the problems that arise have been resolved, it is time to consider overnight visitation.

OVERNIGHT VISITS

The first overnight visit should be a natural extension of the expanded visits just described. As with all new situations, this one comes with some new rules so as to avoid potential problems and so that everyone will know what to expect. These new rules, added to the existing ones, include the following:

(1) Locks should be placed on bedroom doors and used at night so as to reinforce the principle of privacy.

(2) The offender should be fully dressed at all times when he is outside his bedroom. This includes all trips to and from a bathroom (except those with a single entrance from his bedroom).

(3) The offender should not roam about the house when his wife is asleep in bed. This requires that he retire at the same time as or before his spouse and arise at the same time as or after she does.

(4) If he should have reason to get out of bed during the night, he should fully awaken his spouse and inform her of what he is doing.

The return of the offender to the home for overnight visits means that he and his spouse are likely to engage in sexual intimacy in the home. Care should be taken that this be done in a way to avoid traumatizing the victim, bringing back memories of her sexual abuse. For example, if the victim's bedroom adjoins that of her parents, hearing the sounds of her parents engaged in sexual intimacy while lying in the next bedroom may be uncomfortable for her. Some rearranging of rooms may be in order.

As with all new situations, there should be an opportunity for all members of the family, especially the victim, to debrief with their respective counselors before moving on to more overnights. This is a testing period, and it is necessary to allow some time to see how the test is progressing. Assuming it is progressing well, regular overnight visits could then be scheduled. For example, the family could plan that the offender will regularly spend one weekend evening and night at the home. If these go well, the schedule could then include some additional nights at home, for example, Friday through Sunday or an additional weeknight to allow everyone to get used to the offender being at home on work and school nights. Finally, after a lot of groundwork has been laid and the family members have had a good deal of practice with the offender back in the family routine, it is time for him to move home.

THE MOVE HOME

The offender's move home should be a carefully planned affair, and all of the procedures mentioned above are designed to make it so. The earlier rules should, of course, remain in place. The plan to have him gradually reintegrate into the family routine should provide an opportunity for any unexpected problems to appear and to be resolved. The idea is to have his return to the home *succeed* rather than fail. Problems associated with his full-time involvement in family life are to be expected. These will need to be worked out. There is still the possibility, however, that it may be necessary for him to move back out if problems arise that could be best dealt with if he were not at home.

IN DEFENSE OF "RULES"

One obvious aspect of the plan outlined above is the inclusion of explicit and structured rules of behavior. These rules are not quite the same as those in most families. These rules can be awkward and inconvenient and a reminder of past problems. As such, some may wish to put them aside as soon as possible and return to a more comfortable and normal situation. The problem is that incestuous families are not normal families, and child molesters are not normal fathers. All families have rules about appropriate and proper conduct, many of them unstated or implicit. In the case of offenders and their families, those rules were not sufficient to prevent the offender from committing sexual assaults.

In the case of the incest offender, a combination of his sexual arousal to a child and insufficient automatic rules (i.e., internal controls) provides the attraction and the opportunity for sexual abuse. The offender, then, should be thought of as having a handicap requiring additional, explicit behavioral rules to prevent reoffense. These rules also provide a context within which all other members of the family can know what to expect, thus reducing their anxiety about potential uncomfortable situations. The rules will be comfortable for all to the extent that the offender accepts responsibility for following them and understands their importance. This creates a climate where the rules are regularly practiced and become a part of the family routine.

Over time, some of the external rules can be relaxed as they are replaced by internal rules that the offender and the family build into their daily lives. One lifelong, absolute, and nonnegotiable rule that a child molester should never relax is that he should never be alone in a supervisory relationship with a child who is the same sex and in the same age range as a previous victim. Relaxation of other rules should be done very carefully. It should be remembered that the scenario for the typical reoffense is as follows: A few years after the end of treatment and supervision, a series of situations develop where the rules are seen to be a gross inconvenience. The rules begin to erode for reasons of expediency. There is a belief that the offender could not reoffend, having learned his lesson too well. He finds himself with opportunities to be alone with potential victims, and he experiences some sexual arousal, which he keeps secret, convincing himself it is of no significance. Therefore, he does nothing to counter this arousal as it grows in frequency and intensity. Finally, he reoffends. The victim, in this situation of deteriorating rules and unclear expectations, is just as vulnerable as in the case of the earlier offenses.

The process of reuniting incest offenders with their families is a challenging one. Because of the special handicaps of the offender and the special needs of the victim(s) and other family members, reunification requires a lot of work and a good deal of time to accomplish. It needs to be approached with the prevention of reoffense as a paramount goal.

Although there are several issues that determine whether and how quickly and comfortably the reunification process can proceed, the most important factors are (a) the amount of damage to the victim and the family fabric caused by the abuse and (b) the extent to which the offender accepts responsibility for his abuse, the problems he caused, and the need to repair the damage and prevent reoffense. These challenges can be met, however, and can be overcome gracefully and successfully.

Appendix

The Appendix contains outlines of the following chapters:

These outlines are indexed to the text for use as a quick-reference guide.

CHAPTER 4: THERAPIST QUALIFICATIONS

I. *Academic Qualifications* (see pages 34-36)
   A. Education as only a base for specialized knowledge
   B. Relevance of education to the treatment of sexual offenders
   C. Extra-academic sources of knowledge
      1. Workshops and seminars
      2. Professional journals
II. *Clinical Experience* (see pages 36-39)
   A. Clinical experience at the heart of a therapist's qualifications — academic training alone not a substitute
   B. Sources of experience
      1. Work with involuntary clients
      2. Institutional experience with sex offenders
      3. Community-based agency experience
      4. Community-based private practice
   C. Measures of depth of necessary experience
      1. Program characteristics
      2. Work duties performed
      3. Treatment modalities used
      4. Hours of training received

III. *Specialized Knowledge.* The areas of expertise not normally encountered in general practice that are required for treating sex offenders (see pages 39-47)
   A. Sexual deviancy and offender issues
      1. Deviant arousal patterns
      2. Arousal support mechanisms
      3. Methods for altering arousal
   B. Victimization issues
      1. Relevance to offender treatment
      2. Decisions regarding reunification
      3. Protection of the victim
   C. Criminal justice issues
      1. Knowledge of the system
      2. Knowledge of local resources
      3. Acquiring information from the system
   D. Community resources
      1. Victim services
      2. Community protection agencies
      3. Other offender therapists
      4. Testing resources
      5. Substance abuse programs
      6. Employment services
      7. Housing services
      8. Financial resources
IV. *Skills and Qualities.* The personal qualities and skills essential to effective treatment of sex offenders
   A. Dealing directly with offenders (see pages 47-52)
      1. Assertiveness
      2. Confrontiveness
      3. Ability to avoid manipulation
   B. Dealing with the community (see pages 52-54)
      1. A team treatment orientation
      2. Dealing with confidentiality
      3. Concern for community safety
   C. Personal traits and abilities (see pages 54-60)
      1. The ability to cope with stress
      2. The ability to discuss sexual matters openly (especially deviant sexuality)
      3. The ability to be precise (detective work)
      4. The ability to maintain objectivity
      5. The ability to remain realistic about sex offenders (their potential for reoffense)
      6. Freedom from a deviant/criminal history

CHAPTER 5: THE SEX OFFENDER EVALUATION REPORT

I. *Basic Principles.* Four basic principles to follow when reviewing a sexual deviance evaluation (see pages 61-65)
   A. Objectivity
   B. Thoroughness
   C. Evaluations must precede therapy
   D. Skepticism
II. *The Offense Behavior.* Six key elements to be covered in describing the offense
   A. Antecedent behaviors (see pages 65-71)
       1. The degree of risk taken by the offender
       2. How proximity to the victim was gained
       3. Whether any material resources played a part in the offense
       4. What grooming behaviors occurred
           a. physical grooming of the victim
           b. psychological grooming of the victim
           c. grooming of the community
           d. victim issues
   B. Victim elements (see pages 71-73)
       1. How the therapist will assist in planning for the future safety of the victim
       2. How the choice of victim illuminates the offender's pathology
       3. How the offender harmed the victim
       4. How the therapist resolves discrepancies between the offender's and the victim's statements
   C. Significant others (see pages 73-74)
       1. Other family members
       2. Significant relatives, employers, friends, and so on
       3. Other therapist/counselors for the offender and/or the victim
       4. Clergy and religious counselors
   D. Elements of the offense (see pages 74-76)
       1. Is the description complete and explicit?
       2. Are discrepancies between the offender's and the victim's statements resolved by the therapist?
       3. Is the degree of force used by the offender discussed clearly?
       4. Is any psychological coercion clarified?
       5. Is the resistance of the victim described?
       6. Are significant details about the offense unaccounted for in the report?
       7. Are unique circumstances of the offense discussed?
   E. Other deviant behaviors (see pages 76-77)
       1. Reveal patterns of offending behavior

      2. Reveal other treatment needs so that treatment can be focused appropriately

      3. Illustrate the offender's and the therapist's reliability for full disclosure

    F. The offender's perspective (see pages 77-79)

      1. Clarifies the offender's general personality

      2. Reveals the offender's candor

      3. Lays the groundwork for the therapist's discussion of discrepancies in accounts of the offender and the offense

      4. Reveals important offender characteristics

III. *Personal History and Social Functioning.* Information that places the offender and his offense within a wider social context (see pages 79-86)

    A. Family of origin

      1. Prior child abuse of the offender

      2. Substance abuse of family members

      3. Parental marital problems

      4. Cultural influences

    B. Military experience

    C. Education, employment, and financial history

    D. Marital history

    E. Substance use and abuse

    F. Mental health history

    G. Medical history

    H. Criminal justice history

IV. *Sexual History.* Requires complete details in a variety of areas when not covered elsewhere in the report (see pages 86-87)

    A. Childhood sexual experiences

    B. Patterns of sexual behaviors

    C. Frequency of sexual behaviors

    D. Catalog of all sexual practices

    E. All current and past sexual partners

    F. Current sexual behaviors

V. *Test Results.* Obtained from a wide variety of sources and used in many different ways (see pages 87-90)

    A. Most common tests

      1. Personality assessments

      2. Psychological tests

      3. Polygraph tests

      4. Penile plethysmograph tests

    B. Tests are valuable

      1. Weigh the consistency of information

      2. Identify special problems

      3. Indicate the validity of an offender's presentation of himself

    C. Polygraph examination
       1. Measures validity of the offender's report
       2. Identifies inconsistencies needing further exploration
       3. Elicits new information previously unreported
       4. Relies on licensed and trained examiners
    D. Penile plethysmograph
       1. Provides a baseline of offender arousal patterns
       2. Reveals areas of offender self-deception
       3. Identifies new or potential problems
VI. *Conclusions and Recommendations* (see pages 90-97)
    A. Should review critical issues previously identified
    B. Should identify the offender's resources and risk factors
    C. Should include *Diagnostic and Statistical Manual* diagnosis
    D. Should make treatment plans explicit and detailed
    E. Should include what external controls will be used to reduce risk factors
    F. Should logically follow from the content of the report
    G. Should specify that conditions should change only with the concurrence of all parties
    H. Potential problem areas should be described
VII. *Treatment Conditions.* Lists typical conditions for community-based treatment (see pages 91-93)

CHAPTER 6: TREATMENT ISSUES, METHODS, AND MEASURES OF EFFECTIVENESS

  I. *Controls* (see pages 94-96)
    A. Issues: Offenders have insufficient controls to prevent offending
    B. Treatment: Impose external controls while building internal controls
    C. Measure: Spot check and corroborate compliance
  II. *Defenses* (see pages 96-97)
    A. Issues: Offenders reluctant to acknowledge deviant history
    B. Treatment: Confront defense mechanisms
    C. Measure: Client self-report compared to other sources
  III. *Deviant Sexual Arousal* (see pages 97-99)
    A. Issues: Arousal to deviant sexual stimuli
    B. Treatment: Cognitive and behavioral reshaping of sexual arousal
    C. Measure: Self-report compared to physiological test results
  IV. *Cognitive Distortions* (see pages 99-100)
    A. Issues: Thinking errors that support offending
    B. Treatment: Thinking errors identified, confronted, and changed
    C. Measure: Changes in belief statements, corroborated by significant others

CHAPTER 7: REUNITING INCEST OFFENDERS WITH THEIR FAMILIES

IV. *Family Outings* (see pages 114-115)
  A. Time-limited, trial affairs
  B. End visit if child uncomfortable
  C. Opportunity for offender and victim to debrief with therapists between meetings
  D. Rules for family outings
V. *Visits Home* (see pages 116-118)
  A. Follow several successful family outings
  B. Rules for home visits
VI. *Need for Behavioral Rules* (see pages 118-120)

References

Abel, G. G., Becker, J. V., Cunningham-Rathner, J., Rouleau, J. L., Kaplan, M., & Reich, J. (1984). *The treatment of child molestors* (Grant No. MH 36347-01 and 02). Washington, DC: National Institute of Mental Health.

Abel, G. G., Mittelman, M. S., & Becker, J. V. (1985). Sexual offenders: Results of assessment and recommendations for treatment. In H. H. Ben-Aron, S. I. Hucker, & C. D. Webster (Eds.), *Clinical criminology* (pp. 191-205). Toronto: MM Graphics.

Abel, G. G., Mittelman, M., Becker, J. V., Cunningham-Rathner, J., & Lucas, L. (1983, December). *The characteristics of men who molest children.* Paper presented at the World Congress of Behavior Therapy, Washington, DC.

American Psychiatric Association. (1987). *Diagnostic and statistical manual of mental disorders* (rev. ed.). Washington, DC: Author.

Bagley, C., & Ramsay, R. (1985, February). *Disrupted childhood and vulnerability to sexual assault: Long-term sequels with implications for counseling.* Paper presented at the Conference on Counseling the Sexual Abuse Survivor, Winnipeg, Canada.

Barbaree, H. E., & Marshall, W. L. (1989). Erectile responses amongst heterosexual child molestors, father-daughter incest offenders and matched non-offenders: Five distinct age preference profiles. *Canadian Journal of Behavioral Science, 21,* 70-83.

Barbaree, H. E., & Marshall, W. L. (in press). Deviant sexual arousal, demographic and offense history variables as predictors of reoffense among child molestors and incest offenders. *Behavioral Sciences and the Law.*

Berliner, L. (1977). Child sexual abuse: What happens next? *Victimology, 2,* 327-331.

Berliner, L. (1982). Removing the offender in cases of family sexual assault. *TSA News, 5,* 3.

Brienes, W., & Gordon, L. (1983). The new scholarship in family violence. *Signs: Journal of Women in Culture and Society, 8,* 490-531.

Briere, J. (1984, April). *The effects of childhood sexual abuse on later psychological functioning: Defining a "post-sexual abuse syndrome."* Paper presented at the Third National Conference on Sexual Victimization of Children, Washington, DC.

Browne, A., & Finkelhor, D. (1986). Impact of child sexual abuse: A review of the research. *Psychological Bulletin, 99,* 66-77.

Courtois, C. (1979). The incest experience and aftermath. *Victimology: An International Journal, 4,* 337-347.

Dreiblatt, I. S. (1982, May). *Issues in the evaluation of the sex offender.* Paper presented at the Washington State Psychological Association Meetings, Seattle, WA.

Finkelhor, D. (1982). Sexual abuse: A sociological perspective. *Child Abuse and Neglect, 6,* 95-102.

Finkelhor, D. (1984). *Child sexual abuse: New theory and research*. New York: Free Press.

Finkelhor, D., Araji, S., Baron, L., Browne, A., Peters, S. D., & Wyatt, G. E. (1986). *A sourcebook on child sexual abuse*. Beverly Hills, CA: Sage.

Finkelhor, D., & Browne, A. (1985). The traumatic impact of child sexual abuse: A conceptualization. *American Journal of Orthopsychiatry, 55*, 530-541.

Friedrich, W. N., Urquiza, A. J., & Beilke, R. (in press). Behavioral problems in sexually abused young children. *Journal of Pediatric Psychology*.

Groth, A. N., Burgess, A. W., Birnbaum, H. J., & Gary, T. S. (1978). A study of the child molestor: Myths and realities. *Journal of the American Criminal Justice Association, 41*, 17-22.

Herman, J. L. (1981). *Father-daughter incest*. Cambridge, MA: Harvard University Press.

Hindman, J. (1988). Research disputes assumptions about child molestors. *NDAA Bulletin, 7*, 1.

James, J., & Meyerding, J. (1977). Early sexual experiences and prostitution. *American Journal of Psychiatry, 134*, 1381-1385.

Jensen, S. H., & Jewell, C. A. (1988). The sex offender experts. *The Prosecutor: Journal of the National District Attorneys Association, 22*, 13-20.

Langmade, C. J. (1983). The impact of pre- and postpubertal onset of incest experiences in adult women as measured by sex anxiety, sex guilt, sexual satisfaction and sexual behavior. *Dissertation Abstracts International, 44*, 917B. (University Microfilms No. 3592)

Marshall, W. C., Barbaree, H. E., & Christophe, D. (1986). Sexual offenders against female children: Sexual preferences for age of victims and type of behavior. *Canadian Journal of Behavioral Science, 18*, 424-439.

Meiselman, K. (1978). *Incest*. San Francisco: Jossey-Bass.

Miller, J., Moeller, D., Kaufman, A., Divasto, P., Fitzsimmons, P., Pather, D., & Christy, J. (1978). Recidivism among sexual assault victims. *American Journal of Psychiatry, 135*, 1103-1104.

Murphy, W. D., & Barbaree, H. E. (1988). *Assessment of sexual offenders by means of erectile response: Psychometric properties and decision making* (Contract No. 86M0506500501D). Washington, DC: National Institute of Mental Health.

Nichols, H. R., & Molinder, I. (1984). *Multiphasic Sex Inventory Manual*. Tacoma, WA: Nichols & Molinder.

Peterson v. State of Washington, 100 Wn. 2d 421, 671 P.2d 230 (1983).

Quinsey, V. L., Chaplin, T. C., & Carrigan, W. T. (1979). Sexual preferences among incestuous and nonincestuous child molestors. *Behavior Therapy, 10*, 562-565.

Russell, D. E. H. (in press). *The secret trauma: Incest in the lives of girls and women*. New York: Basic Books.

Salter, A. C. (1988). *Treating child sex offenders and victims*. Newbury Park, CA: Sage.

Samenow, S. E. (1984). *Inside the criminal mind*. New York: Time Books.

Silbert, M. H., & Pines, A. M. (1981). Sexual child abuse as an antecedent to prostitution. *Child Abuse and Neglect, 5*, 407-411.

Silbert, M. H., & Pines, A. M. (1983). Early sexual exploitation as an influence in prostitution. *Social Work, 28*, 285-289.

Summit, R. C. (1983). The child sexual abuse accommodation syndrome. *Child Abuse and Neglect, 7*, 177-193.

Tarasoff v. Regents of University of California, 17 Cal.3d 425, 435, 551 P.2d 334, 131 Cal. Rptr. 14 (1976).

Tufts' New England Medical Center, Division of Child Psychiatry (1984). *Sexually exploited children: Service and research project* (Final report for the Office of Juvenile Delinquency Prevention). Washington, DC: U.S. Department of Justice.

Walker, E. (Ed.). (1987). *Handbook on child sexual abuse*. New York: Springer.

Wheeler, J. R. (1987). *Evaluation of the child sexual abuse intervention services of the Snohomish County prosecutor's child abuse prosecution project* (Grant No. 86-SD-CX-0002). Washington, DC: Bureau of Justice Administration.

About the Authors

Michael A. O'Connell has a practice in Everett, Washington, specializing in evaluation and treatment of sexual deviancy. His first work in the social service field was when, as a Navy officer, he was Director of a Naval Correctional Center. He earned his M.S.W. from the University of Washington in 1977, intending to continue working as a correctional administrator. Instead, he found himself working as a therapist in alcoholism treatment. In 1981, he started to work with sex offenders.

Eric Leberg received his B.A. in Spanish Literature from Pomona College and his M.S.W. from the University of Denver. For 15 years he has worked as a Community Corrections Officer for the Washington State Department of Corrections. Previously, he worked in Children's Protective Services. He has been a Social Work Consultant and works as a private investigator in child-custody litigation.

Craig R. Donaldson is Director of the Snohomish County Pre-Prosecution Diversion Program. This program has served as a model for similar programs across the nation and in Europe and also serves as a model for community supervision standards for sex offenders. He has worked with adult felony offenders for 15 years and with sexual offenders since 1983. He has provided training for both attorneys and support staff of the Washington Association of Prosecuting Attorneys.